RASPBERRY RAINBOWS

BY

Pinkie Paranya

Enjoy life' Rainbows!

WOMAN TO WOMAN

A JOURNEY OF DISCOVERY

Pinkie Paranya

Cover by Wendy Morgan

DEDICATION

I dedicate my celebration of discovery to women everywhere, every place, every age and especially to my friends. I love them dearly.

The road is the same for all of us. We may take different turns along our road, but the way is clear.

We must love ourselves—nourish and replenish the child within us. We do this with a process of discovery as we move along.

As a writer, I've observed, commented and confirmed on paper many ideas we all may have thought, but seldom shared. This isn't for reading in one gulp, but take little sips of it as you read, thinking and remembering your own journey.

Life is made of thunder storms followed by rainbows. It is said there are pots of gold at the end of rainbows. When I was a child, the pot of gold never concerned me. I wanted to taste a rainbow, certain it must be raspberry flavored.

I would like to share my raspberry rainbows with you.

ACKNOWLEDGMENTS

A writer is blessed if she has friends who are also writers and/or readers. My friends give me advice, take the time and effort to critique and offer the support and loyalty a writer craves. Many readers have stayed with me, despite my penchant for switching genres.

Wendy Morgan provided the original painting for the cover.

June Agur, Jannifer Hoffman. Rebecca George (R.L.George), Delphine Nelson, Joanne Taylor Moore, Ellynore Seybold, Debbie Lee, Ramona Forrest, Sandra Smith, Robin Christianson, my sweet friends. Wendy Morgan did some fine editing. I can't forget Melissa Stevens for her expertise in getting this book in print.

I am grateful for all of you in being a part of my life. If I've left someone out, know I love you no less.

Last, but not least, I want to bestow a rainbow of love to my sister, Donna Garrett. Donna has given me courage to continue writing. She believed in me when I began to doubt myself. She is a true friend.

Note: I have appropriated some stories from here for LIFE IN A NUT SHELL. You may recognize some of them.

CONTENTS

SUNNY DAY RAINBOW

Today I saw a sunbow,

or was it a sunny day rainbow—

high up in a blue sky, nestled among

dark, wispy clouds.

It is easy to see rainbows when others

see them.

The thrill is to catch sight of the

rainbows others miss.

MILES TO GO. . .

Questions, solutions, events, sorrows, happy times, rejection, acceptance, losses, gains—these are a part of a life that has endured and stretched into so-called middle-age and beyond.

Where do we go from here? Where do we wish to go? Is this all there is? Is this the end, or another beginning?

As women, we bridge the gap between the generations who had narrow horizons to the generations who have it all—but are we so different?

You may have spent a lifetime caring for your family and now your children have flown the nest, the last dog died and you are ready to do something different. Perhaps you are a widow, divorced, and never married. Here's a heretical thought: What if you are married and want to push your boundaries, do something special for yourself like taking a college course, learning to paint, writing a book, working seriously on your genealogy or maybe your memoirs.. Doing something that doesn't necessarily involve your mate. Time goes so quickly and many of us are left with regrets of a life unfulfilled.

There are stages when we must push against restraints, inner or outer, and forge ahead. Spread our wings, or take those first tottering steps to independence. Find out who you are. When you love yourself more, you reflect that love toward others.

The poet, Robert Frost, put it well:

"The woods are lovely, dark and deep.

But I have promises to keep,

And miles to go before I sleep,

And miles to go before I sleep."

We ALL have miles to go before we sleep.

1.

BEGINNING OUR JOURNEY

MOTHERS

We are our mother's daughters, no doubt of that. None of us ever had mothers like anyone else.

There were the Jewish and Catholic mothers, known for spreading love and guilt over us like peanut butter on a slice of white bread. We had homey mothers who wore their aprons proudly, like it was part of their dress. Mothers who taught us to be little homemakers and mothers who didn't.

Some of us might have had a mother who chose to be a martyr for her family and whose sighs were as subtle as the wind from a tornado. She would let us get away with not doing the dishes or cleaning our room, but we paid for it by her long-suffering looks of reproach.

Did your mother ever tell you, "Never leave the house without wearing clean underwear." This was a precaution in case we were hit by a bus and ended up in the hospital. We might be in a coma, but God forbid someone should see shabby underwear on her child.

How about the long ago dictum of not leaving on a date without making sure you had change for the telephone? That instills a lot of confidence in the dating process.

The last resort of mothers, when they were trying to make a point against peer pressure, was, "If everybody jumped off a cliff, would you do it?" It didn't really make sense and yet in some sort of mother-logic it did.

There were mothers who told us about sex, sometimes before we wanted to know. Also mothers who never mentioned the subject and gave us booklets produced by a sanitary pad company that explained our first periods. We had mothers who baked and cooked from scratch. Some of us had mothers we knew loved us by the things they did for us, but they didn't know how to share a hug or a kiss.

It would be the easy way out to blame our mothers for our flaws and faults, since we were a part of them from our beginning. It might even work to give them credit for our accomplishments and achievements.

But the rational and appropriate response is probably somewhere in between. In the long run, we are responsible for ourselves. We choose the path of destiny we set our feet upon.

After all, just because someone else jumps off a cliff, doesn't mean we have to jump also.

ADVICE TO THE DAUGHTER I WISH I'D HAD

Live your life expectantly, each day a Cracker Jack surprise.

Treasure all the smallest joys—anticipate your prize.

Live life joyously and don't let people know

what they should expect of you. Hens also need to crow.

Sometimes swim against the tide, don't travel with the herd,

or neglect your darkest corners. Fly free like a bird.

Never step on another's spirit, or let anyone step on yours.

Be giving, gentle and loving. Keep your center in reserve.

Don't wear blinders, yet find some good in everything you do.

If I could order the best of life,

this is what I'd want for you.

GUARDIAN ANGELS

As has happened before, I was way ahead of my time. I believed in Guardian Angels before it was cool. It's been only recently that angels have come into their own. When I was about twelve, I realized that there was someone watching out for me on a rather personal level. I called her "Connie", short for Conscience, because I thought that was her reason to be with me.

Had I mentioned the idea, my parents probably would have sent me to live with Grandmother for a while. Grandmother would have straightened out my thinking without hesitation. To her, it was all very clear. One believed in the literal translation of the Bible, the Trinity and every precept of the Baptist Church. One didn't venture beyond that for any reason.

I was guilty of working my guardian angel overtime as I grew up. She had to be appointed for me alone because there would never have been enough time to keep any one else from harm.

Once I was washing clothes on the back porch when a sudden desert storm blew up and I dashed out to grab clothes off the line. Inches above my head lightening crackled and snapped—twice. The first time I only heard it, but when I looked up and caught the full action the second time, it was like when you stare into a blinding light and then look away and you still see the flash and crackle.

I must have stood frozen, until someone tapped my shoulder, urging me to race into the house and safety. Another time I walked home from evening church services along a deserted highway. When car lights came up behind me someone warned me to hit the brush. I went off into the wooded area and waited and heard men talking and laughing and calling out to me. They finally drove off down the road. I was sure Connie had warned me.

Often my sister and I used to swim in canals and irrigation ditches. In those days they didn't use the strong chemicals on plants they do now and the water was crisp, cold and clear. I dove under a road viaduct and swam through a big metal pipe with no idea how long I could hold my breath or how long it would take to get from one end to the other. My shorts caught on a bent piece of metal and I could have drowned, but an unseen hand seemed to release me just in time.

When I was five or six, I discovered a snake curled up in the middle of the road, basking in the sun. Something told me to fetch a gallon wide mouth pickle jar and a piece of cardboard to slide under it without touching the creature. When I proudly took my prize home, Mother was not pleased. Especially when it hit its rattles against the jar letting us know it was not happy either. I seem to remember that my father took the rattlesnake out to the river and released it.

I traveled with my grandparents to Wisconsin one summer. When they asked my mother to let me go the next year, she said no, "if you can't take both sisters, you can't take one." They didn't ask my sister to go because they thought she was too young.

On that trip they had a head on collision on the highway and both grandparents perished. I would have been crushed in the back seat had I gone with them.

For a time our home was in the desert on the outskirts of Phoenix, Arizona, and I roamed up and down the mountains near our home without a care for rattlers, sidewinders, or Gila Monsters. And I never ever saw any.

Yet when I came back to the same area as an adult, I discovered a rattler under the porch of the old homestead. I stumbled on rocks and turned out snakes by the score. I found scorpions in my shoes, but nothing ever happened to me when I was a child.

I attribute this protection to Connie.

Sometimes I think I might have worn Connie out, but I still sense her near. She is maybe getting on in years like me and doesn't have so many things to do to keep me alive anymore, especially since I like to believe I've learned to apply a little caution with curiosity.

That's not to say everyone I knew had guardian angels. My mother died early, my grandparents perished in a car accident; my other set of grandparents went to their heavenly rewards, as did my two husbands. This may have meant it was just their time to go, or maybe since they didn't believe in guardian angels, they didn't have one to take care of them.

Now that I've had a lot of time to think about my guardian angel, I believe the reason some people know they are there and some don't is because of acceptance, faith and the innocence to suspend belief in logical impossibilities. I never have had a problem with that. As a youngster I accepted that someone was taking care of me, someone helping God, that is. I accepted it, never questioning if others had a guardian angel or not. It was part of my character that since I had someone, probably it was normal, and not a matter for discussion.

The more I think of it, the more this seems to be the key. I needed a guardian angel, accepted one without question and believed I had one. That's all it took.

A PERFECT DREAM

Oh, the day was bright and sunny when
I left my home one day.
But I was tired of sunny days
so I wandered far away.

I walked and ran and skipped until
I finally caught a ride
Upon a big pink Sal-a-Mon
floating in the tide.

He said his name was Lonesome Jake and he
lived on Sea Horse Lane
Where swordfish dance upon their tails
and flounders do the same.

The sea is red as jelly beans
and the sand as green as lime,
and mermaids dance the whole day long
and there's no such thing as time.

Where the lobsters dress so nicely in
their velvet coats of red
and oysters all wear sparkly pearls
upon their shapely heads.

When the sea is filled with laughter
and strange music can be found
little fishes are playing
on the Sea Horse Merry go round.

Lighting my pathway home that night
'Till I came to the foamy green
Thousands of tiny starfish lay--
ending a perfect dream.

FAIRY TALES

I adore that lovely video called "Lady Hawk". It is a fantasy about a pair of lovers who incurred the wrath of a witch. She changed the hero into a wolf who comes out only in the night. The witch turned the fair damsel into a beautiful hawk who, you guessed it, flies in the daylight. Once in a very long while they would see each other from afar and cry out in despair.

There was only one day in their entire lives when this could be turned around. Now the details get fuzzy, but it was a great journey and a rousing adventure and everyone lived happily ever after. It was beautiful.

It should be interesting to write romantic fantasy. I have a penchant for that which doesn't compute with my Capricorn nature. As a child, when I first learned to read, my parents gave me a huge hard cover book of Grimm's Fairy tales. It was my greatest treasure. Were many of us nurtured by fairy tales, with knights of old, gallant and charming, ready to rescue us?

If a knight in shining armor showed up on my doorstep at this point, I would probably have to take care of him by spraying WD-40 in his squeaky joints and simonizing him so he wouldn't rust and take care of his horse and--

It seems to me I've turned a corner somewhere in life.

WHITE BIRDS FLY

I watched a flock of large white birds fly by in formation today. They flew together in a loose but orderly fashion. One bird stayed behind, falling farther back. My first thoughts were; he was a rogue, a misfit, a non-conformist, a radical (do birds get radical?)

I continued watching as the main group flew along, ignoring the rebel.

When I turned to look at the stray, to my astonishment saw he had picked up seven more stragglers. He circled around them in an ever-widening agitation. They proceeded in a loose, ragged sort of formation, headed in the direction of the first set of birds.

This provoked thoughts, questions and basic precepts.

1) First impressions are not always valid or correct--don't judge too quickly.

2) To conform to the norm is not always commendable.

3) Concern for the plight and discomfort of your companions--whether it be friends or strangers traveling in your direction--is more important to a few stalwart souls than merely staying in step with the rest of the pack.

It was such a minor incident, but if we give thought to what goes on about us, we can open our vistas to new and challenging perceptions, and sweep out the old cobwebby notions that we've harbored for a lifetime.

2

ATTITUDES & LATITUDES

ATTITUDES

A classic example of attitudes is an old friend (single, male) with more money than he could ever spend, who took a trip to Hawaii. He was supposed to stay for two weeks but came back in one because "the prices were a big gyp, the place was too crowded, too commercial, and no one was friendly." He ate mostly at the nearest McDonald's and sat on the beach all day. He didn't see a thing he was looking for when he made the trip to Hawaii.

Another friend, (a widow) also with a fair amount of spending money, went to Hawaii and sent back glowing reports and reams of postcards of how beautiful the moon was on the water, how friendly the people, how different and good the food was and she wished she could stay longer.

In a discussion about this with other friends, some thought that Carl had the right idea and Florence was romantic and impractical.

In the long run it comes down to who left a place in the heart for enjoyment. I guess that's the basic difference between pessimism and optimism. Someone opens the door in the morning and says "My, what a gorgeous day!" and the other one says, "Yeah, but it looks like it might rain".

It's our choice.

You can go either way

The more love you spend,
the more you've left to give.
The more of life you savor
the more you get to live.

      Life is filled with ups and downs,
      Look for the golds and not the browns.
      You can go either way.

The more you master hopes and dreams,
sprinkled with reality,
the more you learn you are not bound
by narrow-minded mentality.

      Life is a burden, or Life is a joy
      You can go either way.

The more you learn to trust in friends,
the more you look to God in prayer,
the more you realize the earth
is not ours, but must be shared

      You can hide from shadows,
      Or turn toward the sun.
      You can go either way.

SPONTANEITY

"Give me a break. I can't just be spontaneous on a minute's notice." I overheard this bit of conversation in a store the other night. Spontaneity is generally regarded as belonging to the very young. Children are born filled with it. Spontaneity billows out of them, in clouds of whimsy and illogical thought. Children can cry out, "Let's go to Disneyland, puleeze!" at the drop of a hat. As if parents can set aside their jobs, hire a hamster sitter, and take off like Gypsies at the least blow of the wind. This makes perfect sense to children. Because they are spontaneous and we are not.

It seems to go with our culture, a basic, underlying need to keep us even, to hold everyone to what is considered "normal" behavior.

As soon as we begin school, we are nudged into little boxes of propriety, made to fit so we can become decent members of society. Color inside the lines, don't use purple crayons to draw people; no one is truly purple even if you happen to know a purple person lives under your bed.

More and more spontaneity drains from our little minds and bodies each day of our lives as we grow up. Calm down, no need to get excited, it's not good for you. Don't yell so loud, don't shout, I can hear you even if you whisper. Don't cry when you're being scolded; just listen passively to the lecture. Sit still, don't fidget.

As we progress through life, spontaneity is the first of our traits to recede. In our teens, we want to band together, forced by an invisible mind-set that molds us into clones of one another.

Teenagers don't know what the word spontaneity means, much less how to spell it. They are the most regimented, most pragmatic people on the face of this planet. To their way of thinking, being spontaneous means all wearing baggy pants that drag the ground or jeans that explode at the knees and the rear pockets no matter how much parents have gone into debt to dress them well in school. They buy their "uniforms" at the Salvation Army and add extra rips and tears if there aren't enough to let a specific amount of skin shine through. Neither too much nor too little skin is cool and only teenagers know the secret.

As young adults, we are not allowed much latitude to deal with spontaneity unless our chosen profession is a talk show host, a farm equipment auctioneer or an exotic dancer. Many of us enter into professions that squash every last nuance of impulsiveness out; the military, banking, highway maintenance, law enforcement, nursing and doctoring to name a few. Those are professions that despise impulsive, unpremeditated thought processes. There are times housewives get into a blandness rut. I've met some homemakers who think being spontaneous means putting dark clothes in with white when they wash, just because they only have a few of each. They look over their shoulder to see if anyone is watching.

A friend once said, "I'm practicing on being spontaneous. If I like it, I may try it on a regular basis." See what I mean? I think we've lost it.

When we take vacations, we reserve our Motel 6 rooms in advance, wait for breakfast until we see a Denny's sign and if someone says, "Hey, that looks like an interesting little town," we firmly ignore the silly person. We have a *schedule*, after all.

The ones who are always late, who dress with mismatching colors because it appeals to them, who are friends when you don't deserve them, these are impulsive creatures who aggravate.

Some of the most vital, interesting, wonderful people are those whose spontaneity has been mercifully spared. This is especially true as we grow past middle age into our senior years. The females of this species are regarded by the more serious sectors as "perennial teeny-boppers" and given a wide berth at social gatherings. I don't believe, at this advanced age, there are any male counterparts to this happy-go-lucky person.

Spontaneous people are not risk takers; at least they don't see it as such. Getting a tattoo, bungee jumping, buying yearly passes to Disneyland and Sea World are normal for these people.

If you are lucky enough to talk to a spontaneous person, you may see a rainbow tucked around a shoulder, protection, much as we used to say children and fools are protected. However so few of these individuals are spared during a lifetime, I begin to doubt this illusion of immunity.

My mother used to tell me, "The flower that stands the highest, the tree that grows the tallest, is noticed and the first to be cut down." My answer always was, "Yeah, but look at the view it had." Like most of the people I know, I've lost my spontaneity as I've lurched through life, but I'm looking forward to getting it back in my second childhood.

Rotten Apples

"You must not lose faith in humanity. Humanity is an ocean; if drops of the ocean are dirty the ocean itself does not become so."

—Mahatma Gandhi

That seems so simplistic, but when Gandhi was here, the world was much more simple, and the people too.

Yet the thread of truth is there in his words. If you remove the rotten apples from the bowl, the other apples are probably okay. But if for some reason, you don't remove the spoiled fruit, it doesn't always follow that the others will be contaminated.

Eternal optimist that I am, people seem to me to be basically good. If it were not so, it doesn't appear that our world would have lasted as long as it has.

It distills down to the essence of attitude--our attitude toward ourselves and what we perceive the shortcomings and attributes of others. Our attitudes and theirs. But through our ingrained beliefs, are we always right? Might we do well to question ourselves occasionally, or do a reality check?

(I wrote this when I was 12 so thought to include it)

THE LESSON

While walking down a dusty road,

One day I chanced to see

An old, bedraggled, dirty man.

It was very plain to me

That he was just a no-account,

Worthless as he could be.

His clothes were wrinkled, soiled and old

His shoes were badly worn.

His trousers sagged, draped like a bag,

the shirt on his back was torn.

His hands seemed a couple of sizes too large

'Till he bent, without a word

As he straightened, I saw in his hands,

A tiny, baby bird.

Gently, tenderly he put it up in the nest.

The tears in my eyes sort of burned.

For how could he know....this lonely old man

The lesson I had learned.

I MARRIED A JUNKIE

Back in the 50s and 60s we didn't have many labels for little quirks people naturally seemed to develop for one reason or another. Like nowadays when obsessive-compulsive is downgraded to initials OCD and schizophrenic, manic depressive and bi-polar pops out of every pseudo psychologist on the block. I never cared for labels even then.

In the 50s and 60s the word junk referred to trash someone held dear and someone else threw out and junkie meant the person finding immense value and adoring this trash.

My husband of thirty years has since passed on to his just rewards, so I'm free now to be a tattletale.

He kept every photo he ever took as a freelance photographer, and I'm talking boxes and boxes. Didn't matter that some curled up and when they unrolled, cracked in several places or that some had faded over the years so the people were indistinguishable from the trees in the background.

He couldn't own one Phillips and one regular screwdriver, oh no, he never met a tool he didn't covet. Hammers? I wouldn't have wanted a serial killer to ever know where we lived and what ammunition abounded so innocently in his tool room. It got so if I wanted to throw away an old pair of canvas shoes that his little toes had poked through or a pair of pants that I'd mended until the seams were non-existent, I had to bag the items and then stealthily sneak out early in the same morning that the trash man came. If he caught me throwing away a stray board or God forbid, a bent nail that he could have straightened, I was in for a lecture that always put me to sleep with my eyes open so he wouldn't guess. He was so serious I never wanted to hurt his feelings.

He saved old magazines because there were articles he wanted to read some rainy day. Know how many rainy days we get in Yuma, Arizona? He wouldn't throw away old Christmas or birthday cards thinking he'd get back to answering these people some day, even though most of them had passed on long ago and left no forwarding address.

I won't get off the track and say he suffered from hypochondria along with his OCD but if I had seen his medicine closet before we married I think I would have suspected what I was in for. He never threw away a medicine bottle empty or full, even though it might have expired about the time the plastic bottles had been invented. I never saw him take any of the old expired medicine but someday he might want to compare the old pills with the new.

And the funny part was, he was a neatnik and everything had a place. He drew outlines on his pegboard for various tools and they darn well better be put back exactly there. His stacks of ancient magazines were neatly placed in magazine racks, in the bedroom, in the bathroom in the living room. But neatly. He stored boxes of items, neatly labeled, that I didn't even want to know about, and stacked them neatly in a storage area out of sight.

It wasn't until he retired that the full impact of his behavior came home to me with breathtaking force. *He discovered swap meeting!*

Imagine being able to go to garage sale after garage sale, buying up everything he ever wanted to play with and when the new wore off and he could bring himself to do it, he might sell it for a profit to buy something else. First we bought one metal shed and then two and when I complained and said, "Let's actually SELL some of this junk," he assured me many of the items were collectibles and would be worth a pretty penny in years ahead.

"But we don't have years ahead," I wanted to scream and stamp my feet in frustration. Actually I don't think he looked at it that way, he'd accumulated his years like he did everything else in his life and just assumed they would always be there for him to rummage around in.

I often have taken comfort in the fact that somewhere up there he is bargaining and buying and selling whatever it is that angels may want to accumulate and worrying about if he should have held on to something maybe just a few eons longer.

The one thing that saved my sanity in those years was that I'm fairly laid back and worry-free so I take most things in stride. In fact he was a much more orderly and neat person than I will ever be. But then that's probably another psychological label that I will blissfully ignore.

PROCRASTINATION

I am the world's champion procrastinator. I would be a shoo-in for President of Procrastinator's Anonymous if they ever got around to holding meetings and if they ever got around to electing officers and if I ever got around to attending. I have so many things going at once I drive myself into a corner and end up hiding in the back yard plunking on my guitar for an hour, just to regain my strength.

My inadequacy concerning time is an example of procrastination. I am either way too early or way too late. I don't seem to be able to center what I am doing at the present with what I should be doing next.

When are they going to include Procrastination as an event in the Olympics?

Many of us might qualify, and we wouldn't have to be in the prime of life either, which at present leaves a lot of us out of the Olympics.

Procrastination can be honed to a fine art, but unlike the raw strength and ability of an Olympic athlete, a true Procrastinator revels in finesse and understatement. A Procrastinator has to fight ill-humored dullards who never will understand the art, such as those of the IRS, the phone and electric companies and Republicans in general.

What would the world be without people not subservient to time, dates and sweating the petty stuff in life?

PROCRASTINATORS ANONYMOUS (PA)

To start a Procrastinators Anonymous, here are some suggested by-laws:

1) All meetings must be attended except when members forget to hold one or forget to come.

2) Officers may be elected by a majority if there is one or at such time when the majority decides to show up at a meeting, excluding baseball season.

3) All meetings must start promptly at 7 p.m. unless postponed or delayed.

4) Guest speakers must be rescheduled at a later date if unavailable on short notice as calling them the same day of the meeting to ask them to speak.

5) Topics of interest must be shelved until a later date if they are no longer timely. For example, there shall be no more proposals for a Nixon recall. Pet Rocks and Nehru jackets are no longer viable subjects, in the event members have postponed discussions about these subjects until now.

6) There are several more VERY IMPORTANT rules to be added. Table them until such time as a quorum is present, the first opportunity we remember to attend a meeting or...

RESOLUTIONS

Here I am again, just thinking
how much better I could be
If I made some resolutions
to improve the same old me.

To lose weight and promise faithfully
not to swear unless I had to.
I could try to never gossip--
I'm aware it's very bad to.

I ought to take some courses
instead of staring at TV
and cultivate all new friends
who would delight in me.

I might dress a whole lot neater
--clean my house from top to toe
instead of working in my garden
watching flowers grow.

What's a New Year's Resolution
without a firm resolve to do
everything nicer, neater and quit
procrastinating too.

So here I am with furrowed brow,
thinking thoughts with no solutions.
It starts the New Year off so
depressing--worrying about resolutions.

It may be time to renounce intentions--
Most people wouldn't give a hoot.
I think I'll try--perhaps I'll try--
to be more resolute.

GETTING IT DONE

Do we ever finish what we have told ourselves we must do, should do, have to do...and yet don't do. And what guilty pangs we suffer.

What would be the consequences of cutting out even a portion of the non-essentials in your days? You might find you have carved out a time to write, or read that book, or whatever it is that you don't have time to do.

Don't put off doing what you want to do. A friend, in her middle 70s, volunteers at our hospital and another friend has discovered that editing and publishing a newsletter for writers is what she most enjoys now. I have never before taken time for volunteer work, but now I am a CASA (Court Appointed Special Advocate) for children and it has been very rewarding. It has given me insights, patience and understanding that I wouldn't have discovered within me otherwise.

Try a new project—something you've always wanted to. Your family may balk at your not giving them 24 hour attention, but they'll get over it. It's about time to do something for **you**.

little rooms

Is life akin to little rooms?
Is childhood one?
Relationships?
Desires?
Needs?

Do most of us partition off our little rooms
so that they do not overflow
but remain neat and orderly
together with our lives?

For those of us unable or unwilling
to tidy our little rooms,
to pick up debris and unusable trash,
does it build up to an unbearable rubble
in our minds, creating havoc and depression?

Is it just as obsessive to keep
such ordered compartments in our lives
as it is to let it all fall into disarray?

So many big questions, so many little rooms.

CONSPICUOUS CONSUMPTION

Have you given a thought to what life would be without a credit card or the ever-so convenient ATM machine? Have you checked your cupboards lately to peer at the seldom-if-ever used Salad Shooters, waffle irons, Fry babies, all the stuff you thought you couldn't live without?

Men are often worse than women. Their "stuff" is usually more expensive. You've seen the bumper sticker that proclaims, "The man who dies with the most toys wins." I haven't figured out exactly what he wins, if he's dead, but there it is. He wins. Maybe we should go back to the old Viking idea of sending a dead man's possessions out on a ship with his remains and burning everything at sea.

That would clear out a lot of clutter.

Possessions have become a panacea for everything missing in our existence. We skim across the tops of our lives, as if fearful to delve beneath the surface. Inanimate objects have become the be-all and end-all. Could it be that possessions have taken the place of grandmas and grandpas, uncles and aunts, and all those cousins who used to be part of the family?

Some of the displacement of values may come from our mobility. We are free to move where we choose or where our work calls us. When the old folks get too old to take care of themselves, the adult children buy space at a retirement village for them. This, in its own way, becomes a status symbol within the circle of friends and acquaintances.

RVs traveling down the road used to be respectably compact and utilitarian. That usually gave the stay-at-homer a smug sense of well being to imagine the traveler cramped in a little box all winter, cooped up inside when the weather turned bad, entertaining friends on a cement patio under the curious eyes of the neighbors.

It didn't cause any envy or jealousy that way.

Now big diesel pushers wallow down the highways and byways, huge double-seated, four-door pickups pull mammoth fifth wheels with twin slide outs. One hundred thousand dollars is not an unusual amount to spend on a rig, and if the drivers get five miles to a gallon, it gives them one-upmanship in bragging contests with fellow RVers.

All this goes on credit cards, as does everything else--part of our principle of conspicuous consumption.

In the old days of traveling, we didn't begin until we retired. Then we limped along on social security. We were usually a one-check family, since the wife was a few years younger and hadn't received her checks yet. We tented or lived in campers for months at a time, chasing sun and warm climates. We bragged about getting twenty-five miles to the gallon whether we pulled a trailer or not.

When we bought our first motorhome, a twenty-eight foot fiberglass beauty with all kinds of bells and whistles, we traded in our old rig and scraped up the money from our meager savings, rather than go in debt and pay big interest. We kept that motor home for fifteen years while others we knew exchanged theirs every year for a new RV with more whistles and bells.

The twenties and thirties crowd all own ATVs (all terrain vehicles) and head out to the sand dunes every weekend and holidays. It's nothing to see a trailer/vehicle ramp combination pulled by a shiny new pickup carrying two or three dune buggies.

Once we camped for a weekend in a state park near Dallas, Texas. All the members in one family, including a boy of about five, had their own shiny new motorcycles to ride around and around the park roads.

The phenomenon of conspicuous consumption begins with the oldest generation and trickles all the way down to the kids. Every Christmas is fraught with terror that the latest, the hottest, the most indispensable toy will be unavailable for the kids. One Christmas, a shortage of Tickle Me Elmo dolls caused cataclysmic shock waves through neighborhoods. Newspapers carried columns of ads from people who bought the dolls on speculation so they could make a killing on the shortage. In football and basketball that's called scalping and it's illegal.

Remember the Cabbage Patch Doll shortage? I'm not sure parents ever recovered from that Christmas trauma.

The combination of conspicuous consumption with our present need of instant gratification is a bad example for the kids. But that's another story.

I don't have a clue to the solution of owning too much stuff. Our calendars contain days for everything from Groundhog Day to plant a tree day. Why not have a Great American Yard Sale Day once a year and dispose of our excess. But then the people buying at the yard sale would only accumulate more stuff and we wouldn't be doing each other any favors.

And we would probably find a way to fill the empty cupboards with lots of marvelous grinder/blender/cooker /baker/potato chip makers that we couldn't possibly live without.

BAGGAGE

He shuffles alongside the highway
stoop-shouldered, neck bowed
pushing a grocery cart piled high with
precious belongings;
plastic bags, old clothes, nests of
aluminum foil, crinkled and wrinkled
much like the owner
plus empty plastic milk jugs
with dried puddles of green algae
nestled in the corners, evidence of
possessions he cannot bear to leave behind
even if it means not catching that
ride out of town.

Giant motor home whizzes down the highway
a boat on top, towing a small car
with precisely the same paint job
satellite dish at the rear
Honda strapped to the front bumper; treasures
to be defended with insurance
policies, burglar alarms and
a shotgun kept at the side of the bed.
Fearful to leave the concrete highways,
he cannot bear to leave behind possessions.

So alike in our differences.

I DON'T DO MONDAYS

There are lots of things that I will do
to fit within society
and maintain my propriety.
I'll cook and bake and stew.

But one thing that I can't abide
Is the day that follows Sunday.
I've always known that one day
is a phobia I can't hide.

Washday Monday, School on Monday
Work on Monday, it's so true
There's no other day so blue,
They should have called it Dumbday.

What if we just had six days
to make an entire week
would it only make us seek
to find Monday in other ways?

Would Tuesday then be Monday?
Would that seem a total freak
to turnabout our week
To have an early Sunday?

All because I don't do Mondays.

ACCEPTANCE

Lately I've been thinking that acceptance is the key to living life with a modicum of dignity and grace. There are certain things in life we must face and accept.

To do this, take the good times, squeeze them out like a soapy dish cloth. Squeeze hard to get the good full value. Take the stuff you like about yourself. Do you make the most of the looks God gave you? Do you stop and think before you sound off?

Are you caring? Giving? Sensible? Empathetic? Humorous? All or any of these qualities make you a better person and the earth a better place for your being on it.

The remainder left in the dish cloth is sediment —disappointments, illnesses, deaths of loved ones, emotional and physical separations—things you have no power to change. Discard the sediment.

Accept what you have made of your life if you value it. If not, change. It's never too late until you take that last breath.

This, then, may be the essence of acceptance.

3.

LIFE CHANGES

OUR BODIES--OUR SELVES

At one point in my life, working in a dress shop was an amazing revelation of what women think and say about themselves.

We are not kind to ourselves, as we would be with others. We zero in on what we perceive to be faults, failings, problems with our bodies which can turn into a life-long litany of disgust.

"I can't wear horizontal stripes. I'm far too short and heavy." The lady was a perfect size 12 with no perceivable bulges. "I can't wear red. My husband says that's a floozy color. He likes me in pastels." This from a seventy-year old lady who wore prairie chicken colors, all dull grays and browns.

One woman, somewhere in her eighties, with lovely snow white hair, said," Oh, I never have worn purple. I took a color test in home economics in high school and my results said I should never wear purple, and I never have." Others say, "I can't wear sleeveless blouses, my arms hang underneath terribly." "I can't wear anything above my knees, my knees are knobby." The list goes on.

In the years I worked at the dress shop few women ever looked into the mirror, and said, "Oh my, this looks good on me, doesn't it?"

Have you ever really listened to yourself in conversations with your family, your friends, neighbors, a stranger at a bus stop? Listen sometime with a fresh ear, to how detrimental you are to yourself. How negative, how grossly modest we are.

In my time, Raquel Welch, the famous movie star, was all the rage. She had fame, money, children, health, beauty, and, still she moaned about being alone, without a man. She married several times, to fairly scruffy men and everyone wondered why she couldn't do better for herself. Still, she'd rather be with someone unsuitable than to be alone.

All American girl Christy Brinkley, envied by most of the female population for her beauty, now in her 60s, had children, financial security, and when she married a much younger man she admitted being desperate to conceive another child for this husband. It's as if he wouldn't want her if she didn't provide him with a son or daughter.

It is said Farrah Faucet had it written in her contract when she was in the hit TV program, "Charlie's Angels" that she had to get off work by 6:30 to make Lee Majors, her husband, his dinner. Where do these insecurities come from? Did our mothers unwittingly pass them down to us? Must we complete the circle and pass them along to the newest generation?

Look for what pleases you about yourself. Admit your good features, ignore a negative that you can't do anything about. Try a new makeup, wear a bright color, one you've never worn before. Look within yourself to see the beauty, the self-sufficiency, the true you. If you are widowed or divorced and find someone you care about, that's fine. If you don't, that's fine too. There are friends waiting out there to meet you. There are books to be read, classes to attend, pictures to paint, words to write, volunteering to give to your community. You don't have to be alone, and if you are, you don't have to be lonely.

***

Overheard in a dress shop. "Now that I'm older I wear wash and wear clothes and get wash and wear perms. You don't have to worry about wrinkles and everything stays in place. I sometimes wish I were wash and wear."

TILL DEATH DO US PART

In a letter to Dear Abby, a woman writes that after five children her husband decided he wanted a younger woman. She goes on to say that she could have let him go but didn't on the advice of a lawyer friend who told her that the children would be better off with a father in residence rather than in a fatherless home.

In the ensuing years she covered for him, even though the children knew they had problems. When the last child was married, she "let their father go." She claims there are no hard feelings, the war is over. "Who needs revenge when the results are so sweet," she says.

To me, that is the saddest letter in the world. That she could live in a loveless marriage, loaded with suspicions, a total lack of respect going both ways and tons of guilt and resentment and then think she came out the victor... What delusion.

Why would anyone think that a family is better off within a war-torn loveless marriage with wasted years trailing behind like the tail on a kite than in a single mom's care with a father's financial support?

The woman's self-righteous pose makes me want to side with the philanderer. What right has anyone to play God with another human life and hold that person in bondage for ten or more years until she decides to "let him go"? Here you have adults who are miserable for years; you have children who know something is wrong between their parents, and if someone doesn't level with them and tell them the truth, they are filled with nameless insecurities and fears. If someone tells them, they must be torn between love/hate of their father and pity/non-respect for their mother who is living with his infidelity.

What kind of message does that send the children in their relationships? What kind of co-dependency does this force on the daughters? What does it tell her sons? That they can have their cake and eat it too? That adultery is permissible as long as you don't break up the family over it? Does it show the children that as long as trouble is swept under the carpet it can be allowed to exist?

Families go in circles and most of us do not break those circles. What our parents are, so we become.

How much better for the woman to make a clean break, cut her losses and get rid of the bum, take back her life and maybe find someone else or raise her kids in a happy home with no arguments, no fights, no sullen anger.

I can speak from experience. My father drank a lot and had lady-friends. As children, we didn't know the facts, but we heard the arguments at night after our parents thought we were asleep. We sensed the turmoil and anger between them. No one told us what was going on, but my sister and I talked together, and when we grew older we figured it out. We wondered why our mother didn't just kick him out--there were times we begged her to, but she always took him back again. Not that we didn't love our father dearly, but for the sake of peace and quiet and a little bit of serenity, we both would have preferred living with a single parent rather than have them hold on with gritted teeth until we left home.

We didn't feel any more secure having them both there, and it left us with the guilty feeling--that, but for us, they would have had different, somehow more fulfilling lives. And to complete the circle, my sister and I chose dominant husbands to be co-dependent with. It took us many years to rise above our childhood training.

In the past females didn't have a lot of options. Now we have more. Yet not all women have options. I read that in some posh places in California there are groups of women whose husbands dumped them for younger, prettier mates. These women go on about their lives, ashamed to let their friends know, sleeping in their cars, going in and out of the expensive stores during the day as if they had something to buy, wearing their old, expensive clothing, but for all intents and purposes as homeless as bag-ladies on the street. The courts are not always on the woman's side, as most of us believe. These women were spoiled and pampered. They have no clue as how to make a living.

"First Wives' Club", a successful movie taken from Olivia Goldsmith's novel was about that very subject. It was kind of a "get even" story and even as we watched it and knew it couldn't have happened, most of us were happy to suspend belief for a few hours just to feel good about ourselves.

A good idea for a country-western song--*How come I'm good enough to go through the bad times with, but not bad enough to go through the good times?*

That happens a lot. To women. Why?

I clipped a paragraph from a magazine a few years back, containing a quote by Christopher Reeves, the now deceased movie star. It made a lot of sense.

He said, "The marriage license says you're committed, but often you aren't--not really. I haven't seen many marriages that have benefited from that piece of paper. If you're a passionate, vital person, you'd be unwilling to accept compromise in life; you have to know you're living as close to the truth as possible.

"—There are basic compromises, not about who smokes or who doesn't, or who likes to sleep with the air conditioner on. I'm talking about mammoth compromises— when you know you're dying inside, not fulfilled by the other person, neither giving nor getting anything, when you're just taking up space. When that happens, both people owe it to themselves to figure out a way in which they can be free again, with no harm done and none intended."

Easier said than done, especially to co-dependent souls, but there are times when thinking of oneself is not negative as most women perceive the word selfish to be. Selfish is good sometimes. We need to learn how to hold a common ground between selfish and selfless.

***

Katherine Hepburn may have covered relationships the best. She said, "Sometimes I wonder if men and women really suit each other. Perhaps they should live next door and just visit now and then."

I thought of a good country song title about dumped first wives: "How come we're good enough to go through the bad times, but not bad enough to go through the good times?"

OPPOSITES ATTRACT

In a conversation with a male friend the other day, I repeated the old adage that in a relationship such as marriage—opposites attract.

Male-like, he immediately gave me all sorts of reasons why my premise was false and that like attracts like. He mentioned the laws of physics, mathematics, and natural laws. Maybe he even threw in Einstein's Theory of Relativity, but I wasn't buying it.

For every coldblooded, window closing, cover up at night in the summer person, there is a mate who is exactly the opposite. Sooner or later they will get together. For everyone who loves cats, there is a soul mate waiting who doesn't and they will get together. Ultimately they may work through it.

This is not a new phenomenon. At least four hundred years ago fairy tales were invented. Remember the tale of Jack Sprat? "Jack Sprat could eat no fat. His wife could eat no lean. So together in all kinds of weather they licked the platter clean." How many couples have you seen who both like broccoli or both like the juicy, crisp fat on the edges of a charcoaled steak?

For everyone who meticulously squeezes the toothpaste from the very bottom and puts the cover on the tube each time, there is a mate who mashes the middle, leaves it oozing and forgets where he/she puts the top.

How about the simple matter of opening mail? There are variations among the slam-bang, tear the envelope apart, barely missing ripping of contents, and forgetting to save the return address type of letter opener. Then there is the methodical sort who gets a pair of scissors, maybe even a letter opener, and carefully opens the letter so that someone coming along might try to open it again, thinking it hasn't been touched. Invariably these two types are living together.

However there are "over-lappers". I have a dear friend who is a wonderful housekeeper. When you come to visit, her first words are, "Oh, my house is so messed up!" and in truth you could eat off the floor. She always claims that she's an indoors person and her husband is an outdoors person. She hates the outdoors, wouldn't be caught dead camping. Yet, she manages to get him to re-arrange their yard like she does her front room, changing this bush to that side, this plant would look better there, these colored blossoms clash, that tree will get too large for that area, and so on. The poor guy grits his teeth and, to avoid confrontation, moves the yard around to suit her, all the while knowing that some of the plants are not going to survive the move.

This is an unusual example of opposites attraction called overflow. When you are so successful getting the opposite to bend to your way of thinking, it becomes a challenge to push on to greater heights. He should stop her now before she puts crocheted doilies on their car seats and shag carpeting on the floorboards.

That's the sheer beauty of opposites attraction and why it works so well. When you find an opposite, you have a whole lifetime with plenty of opportunity and challenge to change that person around. It never works, but it makes life interesting and that's the secret of a good, lasting relationship.

***

Fritz Perls, the psychologist, once said: "I am not in this world to live up to your expectations. And you are not in this world to live up to mine. You are you and I am me. If by chance we find each other, it's beautiful."

***

When a woman complained she was treated like a maid by her husband, another replied, "What can you do when it's a 90s woman, dealing with 50s man?"

Husbands And Other Strangers

When he died, he took with him the comforting cover
that protected and shielded her since their
marriage twenty years ago. They were lovers,
confidants, friends
until she discovered the crumpled
notepaper in his toolbox.
A harmless piece of paper, a poem
by e.e. cummings copied in the
familiar little-boy scrawl.

She'd never known him to read a poem.
Folded and worn, as though he'd held it many
times. What were his thoughts?
She felt cheated. He had left her out.
As though she were not important
in this part of his life.

Had he so badly needed a secret corner
of his own? Were there thoughts
and longings he couldn't share?
As she felt the comforter that once was her marriage
begin to shred into dark holes
of shattered trust
she wondered:
If he kept this secret,
what else was there?

In the end, he was someone she had never known.

THE SECOND (OR THIRD) TIME AROUND

Remember the song that goes, "Love is lovelier the second time around. It's more sensible with both feet on the ground." Well, maybe.

I wouldn't know, since many widows and widowers I have known refuse to even consider getting together on a regular basis with anyone. Why is that, I wonder?

There are certain advantages to having a mate. Security, both financial and physical. It's not pleasant to be alone in case of illness or if you need help during the night. Social contacts may be another plus. There is the opportunity to be invited to parties and various events as a couple that leave a widow hanging out to dry. Some advantages can be double-edged. I have known widows with steady companions who plunk themselves down in a comfy chair for their evening visit, turn the TV to the station they want to watch, smoke and wait for dinner to be cooked and served.

The only advantage to this situation is that the woman can kick his butt out when she wants to; she's under no obligation to maintain the relationship.

Meanwhile, she neglects her women friends and the support and caring she gets from them because she is spending all her time with a male friend.

I've witnessed good marriages and marriages that made playing with barbed wire hula hoops seem like fun in comparison. Maybe if you've had a good marriage you prefer not to break in another husband. If you've had a not-so-good one, you'd be afraid to try another time.

It could be that after years of living and coping and compromising, you'd just like to lean back, do your own thing. Eat when you want, go to bed when you want, buy what you want, entertain when you feel like it, enjoy the company of friends without worrying about leaving your spouse alone.

When you are alone for the first time, because of widowhood or a divorce, give yourself some time with it before you leap into another relationship. At first it's frightening, but gradually, with your inner strength, a little love and support from your friends and family, you can enjoy living alone without being lonely.

Don't feel pressured to look for someone, as if you are half a person without a relationship in your life.

WIDOWHOOD

There is a circle of widowhood that we seldom discuss. When a spouse dies, the foursome that is now a threesome stops dead in its tracks, no matter how long the friendship has lasted. Widows say some friends tell them bluntly, "I feel uncomfortable with you around my husband now that you aren't attached." Or the widow herself feels uncomfortable and drops the friendship. Who makes time to take the widow to lunch after the husband passes away? Who bothers to ask her to the potluck or the backyard barbecue even though all the available bachelors get invited?

Maybe there is a case for the widow throwing herself on the funeral pyre, sacrificed to go with her lord and master when he reaches the other side so she can continue to take care of him.

In our society that would be barbaric, but shunning and ignoring a woman alone is also barbaric. The worst scenario is that we women do it to our own. We do it to our sisters, even though, sooner or later, we may each find ourselves in the situation.

It's difficult being a "me" where once there was a "we". Not too long after Andy's death I went to a concert with a group of widows. I mentioned "we" did such and such. Maybe I said it once too often, for one of the women turned to me and said with gentle sharpness, "Honey, get over it. There ain't no more we, it's just you." At the time my feelings were a little hurt but then I began listening to myself. It was as if I continued the marriage all by myself. She was right. I had to get over it. My husband of thirty years was no more and even though I will never bury my memories, I shouldn't constantly paw through them like photographs in an old album.

Life is filled with changes. The tree that bends in a windstorm lives to see another day, the tree that can't bend, breaks.

THE END OF THE ROAD

When you come to the end of the rainbow

And you're ready to set down your load,

When sunrise and sunset no longer hold promise...

You've come to the end of the road.

If you go before me, I'll be here,

Comforting, holding you so.

And I promise to follow when my time is up

If you wait at the end of the road.

As the rainbow serves as God's covenant,

So the end of the road is a vow

To wait for each other as long as it takes,

Yesterday, Tomorrow and Now.

The end of the road is love's promise

That everything good never bends...

That however long we're together or apart

We'll meet where the long road ends.

"Golden Leaves--A Hymn to Death"

Golden leaves, slip from their prison,

    The trembling trees release their hold.

The earth surrenders tender burdens

    Giving flowers back to winter's cold.

The Book of Life must be completed,

    The great beginning has to wane...

In prime of life, or yet still later...

    We must return from whence we came.

The lovely rose, alas must wither,

    Summer warmth turns back to cold.

God's gift of life we blindly covet

    ...In search of silver, we miss the gold.

The gold of life is just a lovely

    Loan from God with strings attached.

We must be ready, without warning

    To relinquish life and give it back.

Those who've gone are not forgotten.

    They share the very air we breathe.

They go to God for peace and comfort

    And yet we mortals dare to grieve.

THE FINAL WORD

He held her life gently
within his hands,
secure with restrictions and constraints
of love all encompassing—
from love all consuming.

She felt selfish to resist with trivial objections
compared to the indulgence
he lavished upon her
in dedicated resolve.

Now he has left her, ashes to ashes,
boxed in her garden,
a prisoner to her whim.

He wished to skim oceans
that blurred with the sky,
to be one with the elements,
when he was gone.

She may never release him.
Not from anger or grievance,
but from sheer perversity
of having, at last,
The final word.

. . . *Our Own Worst Enemy*

Sometimes I'm convinced that we women are our own worst enemies. How many times have you heard other women disclaim, "Well, I'm not a woman libber, but..." or "I don't believe in that feminism stuff: we have everything we need."

A few strident voices have made it seem that the woman's movement is frivolous and non-productive. When I graduated high school few avenues were open to me. I'm sure many of you can relate to that situation. As a young woman you were free to pursue your goal as teacher, nurse, secretary or, better yet, wife and mother. The choices were simple and few of us rebelled. I would have liked to be a veterinarian or a forest ranger. I thought the idea of staying alone in a tall tower in the forest, watching for fires, reading, playing music, having solitude to watch nature, must be the most wonderful job in the world. It probably wasn't the best job in the world, but I never had the opportunity to try.

Women have made truly amazing strides for equality in the workplace over the years. Nowhere near perfect, but still, amazing. Women today have many opportunities for expression that we didn't have years ago. None of us should ever put down the sacrifices the women of earlier generations made to get these for our daughters and granddaughters. There have been abuses of the system, men are quick to point that out, but freedoms exist now that our mothers didn't have.

Next time you are tempted to say you don't believe in feminism, check it out to see if you are just parroting your husband or father's words. Think for yourself. That's what any kind of freedom is all about.

Don't make changes just because you are bored with your life. If you are bored, find out why. If it's fixable, fix it. If not, then go for the changes. We may go around again in another lifetime, but don't count on it. Make the best of this time.

In trying to inject a bit of lightness into a sad subject, I had to write this poem.

"After I lost my husband" is a phrase I've often heard.
Did he lose his way or wander off? It's really quite absurd.
Euphemisms are genteel, refined—elegant expressions,
But when people die, let them go, stop this 2nd guessing.

If we're inclined to be religious, they will go to Heaven.
And if they were unsavory, leave their rising unleavened.
Either way you'lll meet again, maybe in a new carnation,
So let them die in peace and stop all the variations.

4.

ON WRITING--
IT'S NOT WHAT I DO, BUT WHO I AM

ON WRITING--IT'S NOT WHAT I DO, BUT WHO I AM

My fixation on writing started when I was about twelve. At first I think it happened because I needed to be "different" from my family. Our neighborhood was blue collar, housewives listening to soaps in the afternoon as they went about their daily chores, husbands coming home from work and turning on the radio for the latest news and then mowing the lawn or chugging down a couple of beers at the neighborhood tavern.

No one I knew ever thought of going to the ballet or the opera or reading anything but Erskine Caldwell, or a paperback western, or thumbing through a woman's magazine and trying out a new recipe or reading the short story.

I have no idea where the notion came from that I should aspire to higher goals in life. Not being the least competitive or a high achiever, I only longed to possess a certain amount of creativity. It was, and still is, hard to explain.

Gradually, my parents and friends accepted that I was "different", and began to encourage me in little ways. I kept a pad and pencil on my bed stand and often flicked on the light to write a poem that popped into my head during sleep or just as I awoke.

Often, when Mother woke me in the morning to get ready for school I'd say, "In a minute, I just want to finish this dream." She never questioned the strangeness of my request. After school, while others my age played in the streets or hung around the house, I found a niche where I could be alone. It was usually up a cottonwood tree in the back yard, where I composed my poetry.

My family accepted this as normal behavior after a while and never asked to see what I was writing. Once or twice I showed them, but they didn't seem impressed. But I didn't write for others, I wrote to satisfy some need within myself.

Words were always a wonder. I always looked up every word I didn't know, especially the longer ones. "Supercilious" was my special word for a while. I liked the way it rolled off the tongue. As I tried out wonderful new words I'd learned, my parents let me know I was getting "uppity", which only egged me on to learn more.

During my high school years I discovered ballet and symphonies and all the splendid dark Russian novels along with Thomas Wolfe, Faulkner and Hemingway. By that time I was hooked on writing and my addiction to putting words on paper has never diminished.

Being a writer makes note taking a moral duty as well as an obsession. I have no idea where some of these came from; however, I originated many on my own.

The common saying is "Don't rain on my parade." I say, "Don't wrinkle up my day."

***

Ad for a garage sale: Remnants of a Decadent Lifestyle.

***

Critics sometimes suppose that if they are sarcastic enough people will mistake it for intelligence.

Water and Words. Easy to pour, impossible to recover.

***

The trouble with life—it's so daily.

***

The problem with being too open minded is...your brain may just fall out!

***

Listening to that bore is like biting down on a piece of aluminum.

Do you have trouble writing spare, sparse words?   It's odd, but sometimes I do fancy myself from the Hemingway no-frills school of writing. Yet I cut my teeth on Thomas Wolfe, Jane Austin, Thackery and Walt Whitman, to name only a few writers who share my love for the descriptive passage. Sometimes words can be savored on the tip of a tongue much akin to a lovely taste of pineapple ice cream or a crisp dill pickle. I have always adored words.

Have you read any William Faulkner or Flannery O'Connor? It seems the subject of southern living makes for more lurid descriptive passages somehow. To me their writing is thick and crusty and satisfying, like a loaf of French bread spread with warm garlic butter. On the other hand, we have James Michener who fills up pages to let us know how much research he has done and how much smarter we will be when we finish his tomes.

Leave it to me to do things backward. I started out writing novels and now am writing short stories. Basically, I am too undisciplined to squeeze words into tiny spaces when I can paint a novel using a canvas the size of my own choosing.

Why did we choose writing as a life-course, my friend?   It is so cold and unforgiving, putting your beloved words on paper for strangers to turn away from. I could spray all my rejection slips gold and make my own yellow brick road into infinity. Perhaps it is merely unmitigated presumptuousness on my part to think I should be in print. I imagine a lot of it is wanting to share my thoughts and feelings with others, even perfect strangers. My writing may make up for a lack of verbal communication I have been cursed with. But why analyze everything to death?

Printed or not, I have to write. It is at once a bane and the pleasure of my life. When I least expect it, something about writing becomes enriching beyond mere words. Sitting in a doctor's office waiting my turn, I saw a tiny, frail Asian woman, at least seventy years old. She wore a long, print kimono and a scarf around her head, and looked as if she had just stepped off a boat from China. A paperback book so engrossed her that I had to see what she was reading. As I bent forward, I was amazed to see the familiar title and cover of my very own book, <u>The Secrets of Sebastian Beaumont,</u> from the Silhouette Shadows Series. Be still, my heart!

***

Oops, just ran over the cat's tail with my chair. The cat and both dogs like to stay in my computer room for some reason, maybe because they are convinced animal hair is so good for computers! My computer probably wouldn't run anymore without its daily dose of dust and cat fur.

***

WORDS ON WRITERS & WRITING FROM EMILY DICKINSON

"Truth is such a rare thing; it is delightful to tell it... I find ecstasy in living; the mere sense of living is joy enough. How do most people live without any thoughts? There are many people in the world—you must have noticed them in the street—how do they live? How do they get strength to put on their clothes in the morning? If I read a book and it makes my whole body so cold no fire can ever warm me, I know that it is poetry. If I feel physically as if the top of my head were taken off, I know that is poetry. These are the only ways I know it. Is there any other?"

***

I am coming to the conclusion that we are "programmed" to various degrees during our lives. Avid gardeners have a sort of compulsive disorder. They must keep everything neat and tidy in their garden, all the while knowing full well that this is a never-ending job as long as the plants grow and weeds pop up and bugs are feasting and grass is growing—gardening is never done.

Same with writing. A writer must be born with masochistic tendencies. Otherwise how could she possibly learn to accept all the rejections without taking it personally? And like an artist painting in oils, the work never seems to be done. Constant tweaking and re- writing is a condition we live with on a daily basis.

Raymond Chandler wrote: "Everything a writer learns about the art or craft of fiction takes just a little away from his need or desire to write at all. In the end, he knows all the tricks and has nothing to say."

"I write because I don't know what I think until I read what I say."
                                        --Flannery O'Conner

William James claimed: "Geniuses of all kinds share one mental trait despite a wide range of individual brilliance. They all possess an exceptional capacity for sustained, voluntary attention." I interpret that as don't always talk, sometimes listen.

OXYMORONS--

Writers adore oxymorons. Over the years I've enjoyed the bite and crunch of them. The dictionary defines an oxymoron as: A combination of contradictory words. Oxymoron itself is contradictory: Oxy is from the Greek for smart and moron comes from the Greek meaning dull. A most famous example of an oxymoron is Military Intelligence. Sometimes they become clichés.

I had a college professor who was a wealth of oxymorons and I sat through his class busily scribbling down his words, smugly realizing that no one else in the class was aware of his genius for tossing off these marvelous phrases. I'm not admitting to which are his and which I made up on my own.

***

. . . I'd give my right arm to be ambidextrous.

. . . Tell me, was it you or your brother who was killed in the war?

. . . "The Memoirs of an Amnesiac"

. . . If I've done anything I'm sorry for--I'm willing to be forgiven.

. . . The best cure for insomnia is to get a lot of sleep. -- (W.C. Fields)

. . . There is one difference between a madman and me. I am not mad.
                                        -- (Salvadore Dali)

. . . If people don't want to come, no one is stopping them. -- (Sol Hurok)

. . . How can I miss you if you won't go away? (A song title by Dan Hicks)

. . .

If you won't leave me alone--I'll find someone else who will.

. . . I wouldn't be so paranoid if people weren't always watching me.

. . . How can you believe me when I said I love you when you know I've been a liar all my life?

. . . I'd be a lot taller if my legs weren't so short.

. . . I'll never forget old what's his name.

. . . I heard something unforgettable the other day, now what was it?

. . . I was born at an early age

. . . They either became extinct or died out

. . . A lot of people might not know this but I am sort of famous.

. . . unbiased opinion, clearly confused, freezer burn, jumbo shrimp,

rolling stop, pretty ugly, working vacation, bad health

-- (Boyd's World)

Nietzsche—my favorite philosopher. How direct and unquestioning his principles, how absolute and invariable his outlook on life. He seems to minutely dissect and set aside each gem of an idea in neat little compartments. How I envy the orderliness of his mind. Would he, I wonder, be the same if he were not German? What if he were born in Iran or China or Spain, for example?

"The less you have of possessions, the less you are possessed." One of my favorite quotes from Thus Spake Zarathustra.

***

As writers, we tend to play with words. Have you thought of the two words, Utopia and Ghetto and what thoughts they convey?

Utopia: Greek for no place—not in existence. We have interpreted it to mean a place of perfection that never exists.

Ghetto: A place where a person is forced to live because of economic, legal or social pressures.

Might we be burdened with Utopias and Ghettos as a state of mind? Both are places that exist to torment humankind. One is unattainable, the other seems predetermined.

As we search for a special point in time, a special event to happen in life, and a special place which says "home"—we are eternally craving. We reach for that carrot stretched before us, living solely in the future or mired in the past. We are blinded by a vision of the eternally elusive Yellow Brick Road, always just around the bend or over the mountain or somewhere in our childhood.

If we find ourselves in a mind-ghetto, we can't look back or forward. The journey—if we ever had one—is not across the Yellow Brick Road and around the bend in the river. Our territory is in mudslides and quicksand. Treacherous bogs that turn a quick, sure thought into lethargic, listless inaction.

Both Utopia and the Ghetto can be forever. Only in our minds and with resolve and willpower can we conquer and overcome them.

Writing poetry is a way of bursting out of restrictions, reflecting different levels in life's compartments, something writing fiction can never do. What I felt and wrote about at seventeen is a great deal different from what I feel at sixty, and yet basically the underlying emotions still hold a certain validity. Have you thought about that? Perhaps it doesn't matter, but there I go again being super analytical which is not conducive to a free flow of ideas.

For those not used to reading poetry, try a page at a time. Read it out loud to yourself. When a poet has written what is in her heart, when a stranger reading it can identify and enjoy the word pictures, the emotion the poem brings, getting the feeling of "Yes! That's exactly how it is!" then a poet has done her job well.

I was delighted to see a column in Writer's Digest by Judson Jerome in his poetry section regarding rhymed poetry. Jerome commented that by meter and rhyme he isn't referring to clichéd, jingly verse, but rather he would like to make room for poetry that is memorable, disciplined, eloquent, moving and readable in the form of meter and rhyme.

Jerome said that since the open form is now IN, it is practically an act of civil disobedience to write a sonnet. He quotes author X. J. Kennedy who admires good poems in any form but Kennedy can't write anything that doesn't 'rhyme and scan'. Proponents of free verse claim the old measures no longer correspond with the nervous, staccato rhythms of our time. But why should poets want to be faithful to the cadence of civilization? He wonders. Is that so important in the long view?

There are still perceptible rhythms in the season and times, in the succession of daylight and dark, in the beating of the blood against the arteries. Perhaps proponents of open-form poetry are taking a limited view of the possibilities. That people should think it natural and organic to sprawl all over the page offends his sense of meaning and order to life. (Yea! mine too!) He does not believe that being traditional is limited to meaning conventional.

And so, it is my observation—having written both open and rhymed verse—that there is a place for both of them in our lives. There are times I love the disciplined structure, the creation of meaningful words that rhyme.

Other times it doesn't work, doesn't fit. I refuse to be contained, to be held in check by words. I love both kinds of poetry.

It's a little like comparing Picasso with Van Gogh. How can one? They are entirely different and yet I'm certain if Picasso had seen a Van Gogh he would not belittle the work. Van Gogh would no doubt have been entranced, if a little puzzled, by the color, flow and movement of a Picasso.

Any expression of emotions, feelings (which is the end result of art, after all) should never have to offer an apology or bear the onus of being out of step or out of date.

MY HEROES

I confess to needing heroes

though admit it isn't cool.

Sports and politics are out,

they make us look like fools.

The best heroes are dead ones;

fixed in time and space.

Conforming to expectations

lends a certain grace.

The majesty of prose with

the wizardry of words,

my heroes are all writers

who dote on nouns and verbs.

I do have one small problem

to battle night and day.

Is Thomas Wolfe my prototype

or forthright Hemingway?

Here are a few more notes from my trusty pad that I keep with me day and night. Some are original thoughts of my own, some are from goodness knows where.

Overheard pieces of conversation

.. He's got a photographic memory, but he's usually out of film.

.. Distractions aren't a problem, if you don't let them bother you.

.. Describing a person so lacking in joy: He would turn over a Birthday Cake, suspicious of mold.

.. Overheard at a Senior Center. It's hard doing nothing... you never know when you've finished.

.. Some writers are like cheap wine——.aging into vinegar instead of growing mellow with time.

.. Someone once said: Being a sailor is like being in prison——with the chance to drown.

.. Don't bother crying over what can't cry back for you.

.. His arrogance is only superseded by his ignorance.

.. He's suffering from terminal dumb.

.. She has feelings of deep inferiority——interspersed with delusions of grandeur.

I hope your writing group as human beings are very interesting, but often as writers, they may seem over-involved with trying to live without complicating it by the job of actually writing. They can appear to be bogged down with so many problems. Do they really take time to write? Are they a good support group for you?

Just try to give yourself some space between terminally negative individuals who seem to cling like a magnet for some reason.

A negative person can be shriveling an idea to death in only a few words. If you put a shiny brain-child out for critique, make sure at least part of your group is positive. It isn't that you require warm fuzzies for your work each time you show it, but you do need constructive feedback.

It is hard sometimes not to be negative. It's my nutty notion that negativity is the crabgrass in the garden of life. Once it takes a hold, forget about enjoying flowers, there won't be room for them.

Some people have a way of intimidating people although they probably don't mean to. Actually it's a trait I envy; I doubt I've ever intimidated a single soul in my lifetime. Not even Lobo, my Chihuahua, is impressed when I challenge him.

The power of intimidation leads into my next thoughts on self improvement, which leads me to Socrates and back to the subject of writing again. Thoughts are circuitous aren't they? Do you like that word? Say it out loud, it feels good on the tongue.

Anyway, thoughts seldom travel in straight paths. I'm reading a lot about self-improvement lately. Plato said "An unexamined life is not worth living." But someone else said "What you don't know won't hurt you." Probably Plato's wife. The more I check into what makes me tick, the less amiable I seem to get. Maybe I'd better leave well enough alone. I know why people want so badly to believe in reincarnation. It would be splendiferous to have another chance to redo the mess you created in this life. My answer to reincarnation is: if it sounds too good to be true, it probably is.

***

In a column by Marilyn vos Savant, a writer and intellectual, a letter from a reader went this way: "What can individuals do during their lifetime so that they will have made their lives worthwhile?"

Her answer: "I think any life is worthwhile that produces more than it consumes—whether it's handbooks, harmonicas or happiness."

***

Isn't that good advice? It takes the pressure off most of us who feel an urge to "make our mark" in the world. A thinking person wishes to be more than a ripple of a small stone tossed into a lake. A legacy doesn't have to be grand, only the idea that you produce a little more than you consume. Is that so hard?

***

Socrates wrote nothing of himself during his lifetime. Isn't that amazing?

Why didn't he? Was he too humble to think anyone would want to read his words? Heavens, that never bothered any other writer down through time. Writers have to be a little egotistical or they would never show anyone a word. Was his reticence only because he was by nature more verbal?

Socrates loved to talk, to argue, to ask questions, to play devil's advocate, to expound his ideas to a rapt audience. Could it have been a quirky lack of discipline which kept him from putting his ideas on paper? Perhaps he was unable to think deeply when alone. Maybe it was necessary to have a perpetual entourage to bounce ideas. Suppose jealous writers and scholars threw his writing away after he died.

Thinking from the standpoint of a writer as I tend to do, it seems very odd that he wouldn't have had tons of written words left behind, if only recorded by his pupils.

If Socrates, like Plato, claimed an unexamined life is not worth living, how many fellow humans have we seen who never give a gnat's feather about their unexamined life, and does it impact on them in the end—ever? Are those of us who agonize over what we are here for, who we are, to what degree we have contributed our fair share to the earth and fellow humans, and so on, are we better people than those who sail through life with nary a thought?

Does examining our lives depend on others? The old enigmatic question, if a tree falls and no one is in the forest, does it make a sound? The mind goes on endlessly, doesn't it?

There is a saying, "Accept me as I am, so I can learn who I can become."

***

Enough of waxing philosophical (whatever that means.) You wax your floors, you wax your legs and you wax philosophical. Ye gads, aren't we lucky to be born inside the English language and not have to learn it from scratch?

As a writer, I'm sure you've noticed that the rules for good writing are different for new writers and established writers. One agent told me my book should "sparkle and sing". That my heroine "must be captivating and leap off the pages" in order to sell in today's market.

How many books have you read lately that fit that description? There are some, but it seems as if the established writers are just grinding out the same old stuff. I have begun to like the movie version more than the book lately and that is not a good sign. It has always been the reverse in the past.

Some readers tell me if I'd persevered past the third or fourth chapter I'd have found the book great reading.

How do the writers get away with that when the big rule of writing a book is grab your reader by the throat in the first paragraph or give up writing. Are there different rules for old, established writers than for new ones?

Of course! That would explain everything!

Do you like languages? They are so interesting; I wish I had gone into languages more when in college. German is fascinating in that it seems able to express ideas much more concisely than English. Consider the phrase for a person's twin that we are all supposed to have somewhere, *doppelganger*, is it? That's a neat word.

Want to know what gripes me about romances and why I'll probably never write another salable one? It's beyond my comprehension that every woman reader wants each little sexual detail spread out on the pages. Publishers have become fixated on the idea of what they think women want to read.

We have several Grand Dames of fiction who don't feel forced to write erotica, a polite word for pornography, and they are still writing best sellers. In my book, The Secrets of Sebastian Beaumont, published by Silhouette Books, I had one love scene that was "hot and heavy", but it FIT. I didn't just toss it in because some editor told me there had to be a certain number of prescribed explicit scenes. It will turn around someday and I'll be ready. I've always seemed to be out of sync with the world; my timing is either early or late.

When asked why she didn't read current novels, author Dorothy Sayers' answer was: "As I grow older and older, tottering toward my tomb, I find I care less and less who goes to bed with whom."

Being a writer has its distractions. At one workshop, we were advised to make a list of whom or what interferes with our writing and then try to eliminate it. The speaker said she looked upon her writing as an elephant. She told a story about an elephant carver. He was famous for beautifully carved elephants but he was getting old and wanted someone to take over for him. He tried apprentice after apprentice, but none suited him.

Finally he found a young man who showed promise. He set him down and told him to watch.

The old man picked up the huge ivory tusk, felt it, examined it, and fondled it for a long, long time. The apprentice grew bored and dozed and when he awoke, it was all carved into a spectacular elephant. The apprentice said "Master, how did you do that? I watched and still do not know. What is the secret?"

The elder said, "Son, anyone can do it; there is no secret. You just cut away everything that isn't an elephant."

I'm still cutting away and haven't found my elephant yet.

What if ˙ A lone bandit went into a bank to rob it, left his car just outside the door, motor running, and came out to find a cop ticketing it.

Overheard: "I am eating right because I want to die healthy."

The 2nd law of Thermodynamics (I don't know the 1st one) is "the entropy or disorder of a closed system always increases." Meaning: things fall apart eventually.

Silly idea: Pickpocket with only 1 finger left on his hand can only steal bagels or donuts.

Good cook: She knows when dinner is cooked, when the smoke alarm goes off.

All possibilities exist from the moment we admit the possibility of their existence.

5.

FRIENDSHIPS

To a Friend

I think of you when the day is fine,

when the lake is calm

and the trees are still.

I think of you when I smell the dew

in the early morn

on the side of the hill.

I feel your presence near the path,

I recall your laughter strong and rare.

When I die, let me leave such an epitaph

of a thought, a remembrance, gently shared.

I came across this little poem on the back of an old print bought at a yard sale. It was dated 1923.

> You, Mrs. Fay,
> Always so cheerful, warmhearted and gay,
> Casting your smile around
> Every which way.
> Sympathetic in sorrow
> Tenderly bright,
> Possessed of the courage
> To do what is right.
> The fairest, the squarest,
> Most loving and true,
> Dear little, sweet little
> Wonderful you.

With lots of love, From Stella, June 3, 1923

***

Wouldn't you like to have known those two friends? The sentiment expressed may seem syrupy by our modern standards. The people back in the 20s were not afraid of expressing sentiment and showing their feelings. It's not a cool thing to do in today's world. I wonder if Mrs. Fay and Stella were young or old, single or married, or if Mrs. Fay loved Stella as much as Stella obviously loved her. Was it hero worship on Stella's part? Was Mrs. Fay a mentor or did Stella hold some forbidden love that she had to hide from Mrs. Fay and the world?

***

Much of our confusion toward friendship may come from the mixed messages we get from the media—news, TV sitcoms, and talk shows. I've noticed most women have become uncomfortable showing their feelings toward friends. That is such a shame. I like hugs. I like to tell my friends I love them. Still, there are times when I falter, as if wondering, will the expression of love and friendship make her uncomfortable? We never used to give it a thought.

Gay women may also express friendship toward their straight friends and this, too, could be taken in the wrong context, because of media hype and our awakened awareness toward other life styles.

John L'Heureux says "A friend is someone who leaves you with all your freedom intact, but obliges you to be fully what you are."

Someone said, "A friend is one soul in two bodies."

Loyal, loving friendships are treasures, to nurture and to protect. Where would we be without our friends?

I never used to go to lunch with friends as much as I wanted to. Women seem to communicate more openly when food is involved. The women I know wouldn't say, "Let's get together to shoot some hoops or come on over and take a look at my car's new carburetor system," like men might. It happened to me, so I've noticed with other women that sometimes husbands are jealous of time spent without them and put down the idea of friends meeting for lunch. I no longer neglect my friends. Wouldn't you suppose a marriage and a husband should be strong enough and big enough to contain all facets of a woman that makes her grow, mature and bloom? Often not in bygone generations.

Friends are the garden of life. As with a flower garden, I reap what I sow. If I am kind, thoughtful, loving and nurturing to my friends, good friendships can last a lifetime. This isn't anything I take lightly. I've learned to tend my garden of friends, to avoid letting anyone try to separate me from them.

The true test of friendship is overlooking convenience. When we do a favor for a friend, when we take time we don't have to meet with a friend who needs to talk, when we listen as a friend pours out her troubles because she has to tell someone, and refrain from offering advice unasked for, that is the test of true friendship, knowing she would do the same for us.

When children have left the home, when husbands or relationships change, end, and we find we are alone, we are never lonely if we have our friends.

***

We might give some thought to how we respond to a friend's need to confide in us. If a friend unloads about problems with her children or her husband, just listen. Chances are she doesn't want advice. She needs to talk and have someone listen without judgment and without criticism.

The worst thing to say is, "Well, thank goodness I don't have that kind of problems with my kids (or husband). He is marvelous in every way." Or worse yet, "That dirty dog, I'll never like him again for how he's treated you." She doesn't want that either. She's probably a very loyal person and feels bad enough even discussing the situation, but obviously she has to talk to someone. As a friend, she picked you. So your answers or non-answers are important to her.

We could have the perfect family, but maybe she doesn't want to hear about that now; she needs to tell her story. Hearing about your perfect family won't give her help or support, but only teach her that she can't confide in you, that you're not listening. You may not be aware that you have created a wedge between you and she will probably never again speak to you of her concerns.

Another test of true friendship is when a friend's loved one dies. In the past I've tried to console with the typical, "Oh, your mother was 102; she lived a good long life."It doesn't matter. We are never ready to let go, and such a comment is a very bleak comfort to offer. I listened to myself and stopped saying, "he was better off, he's not suffering." Or "he was sick a long time, and at least you had time to prepare," or "he died immediately, isn't that better than suffering?"

Over the years, I've heard people mention how hurtful these well-intentioned words are. Fortunately, my friends didn't say any of these words to me when I became a widow. Those are not words of comfort, although we intend them to be a solace.

It's hard, but I manage a simple, "I'm so sorry, dear. Please tell me if there is anything I can do." And I mean it. I can show my sympathy by taking her to lunch or inviting her over to my house to dinner. She probably doesn't feel like cooking yet. The very worst scenario, and I've discovered it first hand, is I no longer shove the issue under the carpet.

I make myself speak of her loved one. I try to get her to talk.

When I lost my husband, the hardest to take were the friends and acquaintances who felt uptight about mentioning Andy. I wanted to remember, I wasn't ready to banish him from my life. When I spoke of him or talked of our life together, I felt awkward and guilty, as if I forced them to listen to something that made them uncomfortable.

Being a friend is almost like being married. In sickness and health, in good times and bad, till death do you part. That's a good friend.

A friend once stated: "I have feelings of deep inferiority interspersed with delusions of grandeur."

Capricorn is a fire trapped inside a wall of ice.

People who lead generous lives soon become aware that in the responsible giving of self lies the discovery of self.

***

I had to add a snarky little ditty here:

None of my friends are skinny, why do you suppose is that?
    Maybe there are more important things than a tummy that is flat.
My friends enjoy real food, chocolate, steak, and such,
    They usually don't count calories or exercise very much.

I think it's just a matter of love, they show enough of that.
    None of my friends are skinny—none of my friends are fat.

***

A man said to me once: "It took a lot of years for me to realize that I could wear a pink shirt, ride a woman's bike, shed a tear when I needed to, and still be a man."

***

Caution: Beware of Psychic Vampires:
    Sucking away your energy, feeding upon your soul.,
      They will change your positives to negatives,
        leaving behind an empty hole.

Have you ever thought what qualities you like in a friend? These are my favorites

1) **ECONOMY**. Both of moment and speech. Meaningless conversation to avoid silence is irritating as are fluttering, irrational movements that denote a lack of peace within oneself.

2) **CARING**. An embedded—not surface warmth. Not necessarily linked with a need for self-expression, just there to be drawn upon when needed.

3) **CAUTIOUS SPONTANEITY**. An unselfconscious ability to enjoy something new and still remain in control--to accept certain boundaries of sensitivity and decorum while retaining fresh enthusiasm.

4) **ABILITY TO COMMIT**. Without strings or without thought of reciprocation or reward.

5) **HUMOR**. The capacity to smile at oneself without judging too harshly or enjoying one's virtues too much. To have a sense of the ridiculous, the outrageous and not be shocked or dismayed by the humor of it.

6) **A SENSE OF PERSPECTIVE**. An innate idea of what is of everlasting importance and what is transitory or unessential in a life.

Those are attributes I would wish for myself and strive for, attributes that I look for in others. If a person has even one of them, I am happy.

***

—A friend is a present you give yourself.
—Author Unknown

***

--So long as we love, we serve. So long as we are loved by others I would almost say we are indispensable; and no one is useless while he has a friend.

—Robert Louis Stevenson

***

—A friend is one to whom one may pour out all the contents of one's heart, chaff and grain together, knowing that the gentlest of hands will take and sift it, keep what is worth keeping and with the breath of kindness, blow the rest away. —Arabian Proverb

***

It is striking that when we wish to indicate a peculiarly happy relation between husband and wife, parents and children, brothers and sisters, we say that they are" friends". Friends play together and work together; laugh together and weep together; fight together, triumph together, die together. The word is the very heartbeat of the world.

—Anne C.E. Allinson

PAPPY

Milford Rice was the gentlest man I've ever known. He was a neighbor, in his eighties, when I first saw him, but known as a reclusive bachelor. A small man, barely 5'2", he scurried like a startled mouse when approached, especially by women. Women seemed to scare him to death.

We lived in a mobile home/RV park which was a tight little community within itself. When the residents had a meeting and agreed to watch out for each other, I chose Mr. Rice as my charge. One of the greatest fears of a senior citizen is dying in the night and no one finding the body until buzzards began to hover to alert the authorities. We agreed not to let that happen to our neighbors.

Since I hadn't seen Mr. Rice venture out of his little trailer for a couple of days, I knocked, tried to peer in the windows, and pestered him until he finally came to the door. The previous day he'd hitchhiked sixty miles to the next town to get a cataract operation, grabbed a ride home on a freight train (we weren't far from the railroad tracks) and walked across a couple of farm fields to get back home.

I took him a bologna sandwich and a bowl of chicken noodle soup, the best I could come up with on a short notice. He came outside and we sat on two rickety old chairs while he ate. After that he gradually allowed me into his life.

Everyone had always called him "Pappy". It turned out he wasn't as much antisocial as deaf. He had several hearing aids in the drawer. Same as his teeth. He had his teeth pulled when they bothered him, with three sets in that same drawer. I never saw a thing, from corn on the cob to steak, which Pappy couldn't gum right up without needing his "store bought" teeth.

When he had his second cataract operation several months later, I insisted on taking him to and from the hospital. He always worried about being a bother or imposing on anyone. He said he had a brother-in-law who "got sick" and whose family babied him literally to death. He didn't want any part of that. His mother died when he was four. Shortly after that his father must have suffered a nervous breakdown and abandoned the three young children. It was not a prosperous time on the farms in Oklahoma. Not many families had room for someone else's children. A childless couple took one of the boys. Pappy went to live with relatives who didn't want him. His sister, when she reached the age of fourteen, married and took him into her home.

Trains ran not too far from the farm and he listened to their lonesome wails until, at sixteen, he hopped a freight and from then on riding the rails was in his blood.

Before I got to know Pappy, we often saw him with his backpack and bedroll heading toward the tracks early in the morning or at dusk, and knew he was off on another adventure. Once he hopped a freight thinking it was going to California and he wound up in Colorado before he could jump off, but it didn't seem to matter. He left the trains and worked in the wheat fields, picked cotton, whatever was available. Those were the days before automation and the farmers welcomed extra help from the wanderers.

Pappy called himself a 'bo, short for hobo and prided himself on never begging for food or lodging. He swapped stories at campfires where the 'bos cooked in tin cans and drank boiled coffee so strong it could melt a spoon.

He always wore clean, if wrinkled clothes. We could see him go across the park to the shower with his towel every day at the same time. He was clean shaven and used Mennen cologne when he wasn't hopping the trains.

Pappy never smoked or drank, as many of the 'bos did. He told stories of watching them sift cans of sterno through a loaf of bread to "get the poison out" and get at the alcohol. In those days bay rum shaving lotion had a lot of alcohol and you could buy a cough medicine without a prescription called codeine terpin hydrate. He said the campground was littered with cans and bottles of both.

Once a week we took Pappy out to eat. He always wanted to go to Chester's Chuck Wagon, a local hangout, where he loved to eat chicken-fried steak smothered in thick white gravy, or fried chicken and mashed potatoes. He bought three lottery tickets, one for each of us every week, but we never won even a dollar.

Sometimes Pappy told me about his nightmares. He had very original dreams and remembered them, too. One was that I had put some sourdough in his refrigerator (I made him sourdough pancakes sometimes) and during the night the batter rose and filled the refrigerator, oozed out and covered up the dinette table in the front of his little trailer and was oozing back to cover up his bed as he awoke.

Another night he dreamed that Mexican soldiers (we lived only a few miles from the border of Mexico) swarmed across the border and shot and stabbed everyone in Yuma and the surrounding area. They were just getting to our park when he woke up. He had some pretty close calls.

He told some interesting stories about his early days in Oklahoma and about his travels from coast to coast. He didn't like it back East, thought the West was good enough for him. He was such a loner, such a self-contained person, we were surprised to learn that he'd been married and had four children. When they married, he told his wife, "When we don't agree anymore, we don't need to be married." One day he decided they hadn't agreed on anything in a long time and he left, never looking back. He thought he had grandkids in California, but wasn't sure where they were.

He brought me little gifts from "the Sally" every once in a while. "The Sally" was what the 'bos called The Salvation Army. A handful of bright red plastic roses that caught his eye, a vase he thought I could use, a throw-rug for my porch. He used to crawl into paper dumpsters to recover "almost new" magazines for me until a police car pulled up and told him not to do that. I'd had no idea where he was getting the magazines.

He cooked his own meals until he couldn't see to do it. He always was proud that in all his travels, he never had to "take a dive", which was 'bo talk for going to a mission and listening to a sermon for your supper.

One person he cared for above all was Joyce, a niece in Texas. She and her husband came in their RV once a year on Thanksgiving and we all went out to eat, Pappy's treat. There were times I would have liked to spend Thanksgiving with my sister and her family, but we understood that this was a big deal to Pappy. It was his chance to "pay back" some of the favors given him.

As the years passed, Pappy's sight deteriorated. Early one morning we saw him head out toward the tracks with his backpack and bedroll. At dusk he came home, raised the lid on the trash can in front of his trailer, and threw away the bedroll and backpack.

That was his last attempt to hop a freight. He didn't admit until much later that he couldn't leap aboard anymore. He couldn't see to time his jump. Arthritis had settled in a knee. I felt I had seen a hawk lose its wings and turn into a barnyard chicken. It was sad for the entire neighborhood.

He had one true love of his life. On one of his visits home between freight hops, when he was barely out of his teens, he fell in love with Polly, the small town girl he'd always admired. They loved each other fiercely, but she had wealthy, influential parents who persuaded her, probably rightly so, that Milford Rice would never settle down, never be a good provider, never give her security, and she must not consider him as a suitor. They broke up and never saw each other again.

When he was eighty-four, his niece forwarded a letter from his old girlfriend Polly. She had lost two husbands and wanted to know how Milford was doing. When I read her shaky, spidery hand writing, he had tears in his eyes, the first I'd ever seen him shed. After all those years he remembered her birthday and sent her a card, asking me to write, "To an old flame—the pilot light never went out."

After his rough beginning—of losing a mother and being "discarded" by his father, and then losing Polly, he never allowed himself to love again.

Finally the day came when we had to consider sending him to a rest home. It turned out that he enjoyed every minute there. He used to tell me over and over, "I'm so glad you brought me here." He couldn't hear, his sight was almost gone, but otherwise he was healthy. He went through a large turnover in roommates, which didn't bother him, because he refused to talk to anyone but the staff. The roommate's loud TV didn't annoy him. He didn't hear the grumbling and snoring from the next bed. He never knew that one of his roommates argued with his dead wife all night long. He was insulated in a happy cocoon with good eats and someone to help him shower every day and give him clean clothes. We visited him when we could.

Pappy died in his sleep, slipping away quietly into the night, as if he didn't want to cause any problems for anyone. He had just celebrated his ninety-first birthday.

RIDING THE RAILS

As a young man of sixteen, I gazed out the door,
searching across the farm for wind whipped sails
on endless water with waves as high as corn.
Then I heard the clacking on the rails.

I've heard them all my life but never listened—
the early morning whistle just a sound
as the freight train sped along beyond the orchard.
I knew tomorrow morning I'd be gone.

I rode the rails to 'Frisco and the ocean
and saw such sights to make the country pale.
But nothing satisfied me like the motion
of a heavy duty freighter on the rails.

I hit Idaho in time to harvest wheat,
A rail yard bull in Albuquerque whipped my tail,
I worked the mines in Colorado, cowboyed up near Butte,
No, nothing satisfied me like the rails.

I listened to a hundred stories told at campfires
and told a few exaggerations of my own.
I shared coffee with a thousand other fellers
yet nothing ever told me to go home.

Ripping through the night in an open box car,
with the stars so close you can touch them on your face
your head upon your bedroll, the powerful engine thrumming,
that's when you'd trade nobody for this space.

When I can no longer leap upon a box car,
when my eyes and ears begin to fail
I pray I die somewhere near the siding
So I can always hear the clacking of the rails.

To Milford Aaron "Pappy" Rice, a rail rider. 1902-1993

WHEN A FRIEND DISAPPEARS

One of the best friends I ever had was Jean. There's not a day I don't remember her, not a day I don't think of sharing a joke or a tidbit of gossip with her. Is that a sign of a good friend, when just because she is gone, there is no forgetting?

Jean was at least ten years older than I, but we never discussed ages. We had a supportive, nourishing and loving friendship for years and years.   She was an emotionally battered wife if there ever was one, but she never thought of leaving. Once in the first years of their marriage she did go home and her mother, a strict old-fashioned Swede from the Old Country, who said she made her bed, now she had to lie in it. For fifty-three years she did.

It wasn't that Bob set out to be mean and nasty; it was just his basic nature. He was always negative, never liked the way she did anything. A retired Navy submariner, he was a fanatic for everything being in its place. They lived permanently in a 28' RV, leaving Yuma in the summer and returning for the winter. It wasn't always easy putting everything away each time it was used.

He began to insist on doing all the shopping, sometimes asking her to sit in the car and wait. He took over the cooking, which she had always loved doing. Still she stayed her usual sunny and loving self.

Jean and I went shopping and to lunch at least once a month. She got to spend money on herself, buying her favorite perfume, Tea Rose. Once she bought a bottle for me, but I couldn't use it. The smell belonged to her and not me, but I didn't tell her.

Bob never minded when we went out together. He may have wanted to be alone a while too. We laughingly made a pact not to speak of husbands when we "went out on the town". We giggled like schoolgirls. Jean was tall and slender, almost angular. But she enjoyed eating, always ending up with coffee and a huge banana split. I'm sure the waitresses had side bets that she couldn't eat it all, but she did, every morsel.

At those times she was the Sodaburgh girl, a small town Swede with a sweet face and open, generous nature, instead of a woman in her seventies. I could see her as that laughing pretty young girl in the photo she brought out to show me. I always pretended I'd never seen it before.

She got a kick out of introducing me to waitresses and sales clerks as her daughter. As far as I know, those simple jaunts were her only bright spots. With the passing years, her husband grew more and more restrictive and negative.

I sent her "almost mother's day" cards every year, when they left for the summer, remembering her birthday when no one else did. When I tried to give her some little thing for Christmas, Bob made her give it back, said they didn't give or receive gifts. She brought the gifts back with tears in her eyes and always said, "we don't have room for this". We knew why she couldn't keep a gift, but it was enough that I offered it. She loved roses and music so much. Once I gave her a small music box with roses in a glass on top that turned round and round. It was such a small, delicate object, I felt sure he'd let her keep it. She hugged it to her bosom and cried. Silently, she handed it back to me, shaking her head. When she came to visit, I took it out for her to hold and turn the key to play the song. I haven't been able to part with it.

As the years passed, Jean began to slowly move away, hiding sometimes for days in a place where no one could go. During these times, I'd look into her eyes, and it was chilling to see that Jean wasn't there. Then days would come when she was her old self again.

One day it came to me in a flash that my Jean wasn't at home anymore. I looked into her pretty blue eyes and saw a stranger, a sometimes hostile, sometimes pathetic stranger who stole in while no one looked and took over her body and soul.

I begged Bob to take her to a doctor. They had insurance, but he harbored a deep distrust of doctors and wouldn't hear of it. He said nothing was wrong with her. When she thought something was definitely wrong with him physically, he wouldn't think of going for himself, either.

Jean became hard to manage. She was incontinent, judging by the stacks of laundry Bob did every day. She wandered off and once walked two miles down the road before he remembered to look for her. One time the neighbors must have complained to the police. I think he knew something was terribly wrong by then and was willing to get her into a place to be checked, but the sweet, easily-led Jean had gone and the surly stranger who took her place refused to go anywhere. The officers said unless she was a proven danger to herself or others, they could not take her away without her signed permission.

So Bob was caught in a dilemma of his own making. When he could have taken her for help, and she would have gone with him, he refused. Now she wouldn't go anywhere with him and he didn't dare leave her alone. I "baby-sat" sometimes when he had to go shopping. He couldn't leave her in the car alone and she was like an unruly child to take inside the grocery store.

She came to my house almost every day to beg me to drive her to her sister's in San Diego. Her sister had been dead for years, but she did have some remote family there. She would hold out a handful of coins as if they had been silver dollars, offering the money if I would take her away. I have to admit that I sometimes did lose patience when I saw her walking down the road toward my house for the tenth time the same day, to ask if I would take her to San Diego. She was obsessed with leaving. I always wondered if Bob was mean to her to make her want to leave. She would have been the only one to say, and she couldn't. Once Bob said he caught her at the medicine cabinet putting lipstick all over her face. He asked her why she did it and she said her face hurt.

Then one morning Bob drove to my house, and called me outside. His expression, usually cool and aloof, showed desperation and despair. He wanted to leave a sealed envelope with me and I wasn't to open it until the next day. He made me promise. I asked him if I could help. He said no, he suspected he had cancer of the bladder or prostate and he didn't want treatment. If he died he didn't want to leave Jean alone to be put away in storage at some nursing home for strangers to care for. He asked if I would see to it that she got care from her nieces.

I felt something tug at my heart and knew he wasn't telling everything. If he died suddenly, what would happen to Jean? I didn't think her family was very close. Even though they had not been friends during their marriage, they were bound together with an unbreakable cord. What would one do without the other?

He refused any comfort I tried to offer and shrugged off my clumsy attempt at sympathy. At the same time my heart went out to him, I felt frustrated anger that after fifty-three years together, this was the best he could do. This man had always lived a self-centered, insulated existence. He didn't like or trust people; Jean had been his buffer against the world.

Typically selfish to the end, he instructed me hold the envelope and not to tell anyone about it. I had a hard time holding back tears. I felt that something terrible was about to happen. His expression was stony, withdrawn. I wish I could believe he'd already used up his tears, but maybe he never had any.

Life held nothing more for either of them. At best, if he could have accepted help from anyone, there stretched out a future of hospitals, nursing homes, and loneliness. They had no family to speak of. Neither ever mentioned brothers nor sisters all the while I'd known them and they never had children. If he had cancer and died before Jean, the thought of leaving her alone, helpless, must have been intolerable. Belatedly, and for once in his married life, he worried about what would happen to her without him.

I asked him what he was going to do. I told him I suspected he had made a decision and it wasn't the right one. As a friend, what was the best thing for Jean? Was he going to end his life? If I called 911 and someone came out to stop him, would he only do it anyway later? The authorities hadn't been of any support when he called on them before to help them.

Much of life is spent in indecision and letting things happen. I'd lived my whole life that way. I hugged him and he left.

Later that day we heard the sound of muffled shots and somehow I already knew they both had found peace.

Jean, friend of mine

Jean, friend of mine, where did you go?

I look into your once bright eyes

the color of a Minnesota sky

and you are not there.

I need to think of you as not gone

but living in a secret world

to which you have escaped without me.

I miss your friendship,

knowing you no longer care.

Your once sharp wit is dulled,

your laughter stilled, your gentleness gone.

Are they with you, hiding in your secret place?

The essence that was you

no longer lives within your body,

or yet behind that mask you wear to trick us.

You are a missing person; a missing soul.

The question begs the answer

you can never give.

Where did you go?

From a letter to a friend.

It's hard to know what to tell a person for comfort when she says her life has been for nothing.   Also sad that as a writer there comes a feeling of inadequacy sometimes, that with a plethora of words at our fingertips everything worth saying dissolves into clichés if spoken?

A person has accomplished much in a lifetime, if your offspring have never robbed banks nor shot at the President. If you have dear grandchildren who adore you and many friends who love you because you have always done good things for people or a house full of cats who adore you.

It used to bother me about leaving a vacuum behind when I died, but I think that if we are remembered lovingly and with a smidgen of remorse by friends and relatives left behind, that is about all we can ask for.

And it should be enough.

WILD BILL

I have to warn myself from time to time to be cautious about destroying a sense of fun and adventure. Some of the most interesting people I've known were probably not "socially acceptable".

Have you ever known someone who intrigued you, fascinated you, yet deep down inside you wouldn't want to introduce that person to your closest friends? There's a bit of a snob in each of us, I suppose.

Wild Bill was such a man. He dropped in at our little refrigerator repair business and sat down as if prepared to stay the rest of his life. A big, strong looking man, he must have weighed 225, and was at least 6'4". His hands were huge, with fingers like sausages.

He never deigned to tell us his name, but when I pressed him for one, he said to call him Wild Bill. He claimed names, like ages, weren't a reality, but only labels society tacked on to pigeonhole us. I just thought of him as Bill, which made him more acceptable to my more conservative standards. It was also his contention that there was no such thing as insanity as we knew it, merely labels, again, that society tacked onto us.

I thought he might know a bit more about this subject of insanity than I was willing to let him delve into. He wore a once expensive white Stetson with all kinds of fishing lures and pins, everything he could find on his travels, and I could tell he'd been a lot of places. He seemed clean, although he looked as if he'd thrown his clothes on as an afterthought and wore pretty much of what he owned, which meant he could have been homeless and had nowhere to leave his things.

I wanted to straighten his collar; one side of it usually stood at attention against his neck. He had a fairly trimmed white-gray beard and mustache. Once I made a tactical error of offering him cookies and coffee. When he finished eating his cookies, he took a comb from his pocket and meticulously combed crumbs from his mustache and beard.

He could have been sixty, he could have been eighty. It was hard to tell, but once he took off his hat and we saw he had a full head of white hair. He took a liking to us. I got the impression he didn't suffer fools and had little patience with the majority of the populace. Maybe he appreciated our company because we accepted him as he was without judging him. And we were good listeners.

Wild Bill discoursed at length on physics, aerodynamics, medicine, and politics. Politics was an especially dicey subject. He wanted all the "antique duffers" in Congress wiped out to start over with a new batch. His fury sometimes built up when he was on a particular subject and his bushy eyebrows were ferocious caterpillars above his fierce black eyes. It would have sent any child rushing down the street and didn't do too much for my peace of mind either.

He made outrageous statements and often I remembered to look up some of them in my encyclopedia after he left. He was always right on the money. He admitted to being a speed reader, with no patience for fiction or novels.

He didn't visit us every day. Luckily most of our business was over the phone or my husband wouldn't have let him sit in our office as if he were a full partner.

At the time of Wild Bill's visits, I was in my late twenties, kept journals, and he became a fascinating object of my budding writer's interest. My husband warned me Bill might be a serial killer or escaped convict, but in my immature wisdom, I figured Wild Bill didn't appear to be hiding out in that get-up, so why worry.

I could have learned a lot more from Wild Bill, but he tolerated no exchange of ideas. In looking back, I think he liked to visit me because I was overwhelmed by his personality and listened to him with rapt attention. His visits let me peek into his disordered, possibly mentally disturbed world and what I did learn was even though someone dresses differently and acts outside society's norms, we can still give that person respect.

We never knew what happened to him. One day Bill was there, the next week I found a long stemmed rose on my desk but never saw him again.

Now, in my mature wisdom, I would probably not let any one like Wild Bill in my front door. He could actually be a serial killer or escaped convict, at the very least manic-depressive, possibly schizophrenic with a large dash of paranoia thrown in.

Labels. We learn to put on labels as we go through life. Instead of broadening our views as we grow older, we narrow down and let our fears guide us. We are afraid that our friends and neighbors will think us odd, will not approve, and will laugh if we let the outrageous show in our lives.

I would have missed a lot had I never met Wild Bill.

SISTERS

Sisters are a rare commodity. We get to see at once a mirror and an opposite of ourselves. Sometimes when sisters are too much alike it takes years of growing up for them to become friends. Sadly, some sisters never reach the point of friendship.

As a writer, I should be able to write about the subject of sisters with objectivity, but I can't. I love my sister. Donna is generous, thoughtful, bossy, sensitive, caring. Did you notice how I sneaked in the "bossy" part? That is at once an endearing and exasperating quality. Endearing because she cares enough to boss me around, or tries to. Exasperating, because I am the elder and it is my place to boss if I wished to. Which I don't. So she does.

With my four year edge on her, I seemed to grow up and away. I wasn't there for her when she needed a big sister. I owe her a lot for forgiving me. I was a terrible role model. To her everlasting credit, she has never chastised me and that, too, carries a burden of guilt that I'm working through.

While we grew up, I, as older sister, took the lead. I was a consummate tomboy but she never was. Still, she tried to climb trees, falling out at every turn. She had a habit of sticking her tongue out when she wanted to do something difficult and while she tried to follow me as I played Tarzan swinging from limbs, she fell out of the tree and nearly bit off her tongue. She still has the scar. I got a good spanking for leading her on that caper.

I was a relentless tease and she had no sense of humor--a bad combination. What she lacked in humor she made up for in temper. She was awesome when I pushed her over the edge. Once she chased me with a broom and when I crawled under a bed to hide, she knelt down and shoved the broom in on me. Once she hit me directly on the arm with a wire-haired brush and I carried four rows of tiny dots around for weeks until it faded away. I never told on her because I knew I had pushed too far with my teasing and I would get in trouble too.

Four years older, I was scared of her and yet, the next day I would be teasing all over again. What I lacked in positive role modeling I made up for in the "don't do what I do or you'll be sorry" department. I was forever challenging authority, something that did not sit well with our father. Those were the days when you did what you were told without asking why. I always had to know why. Most of my spankings were because of this. When we were growing up, spare the rod and spoil the child was on the par with take this tablespoon of castor oil and it will cure whatever ails you, from warts to appendicitis.

Every parent did it. When I got switched on my legs with a thin branch from our cottonwood tree, my sister watched, listened and learned not to do the same thing or ask the same questions. Once I talked her into crossing a graveyard at night and then made up scary noises and pretended to run away from her. I'm not proud of myself. My only excuse is that I was young and stupid with a warped sense of humor.

But we had good times together. Life was not so complicated in those days. In our conservative, middle class neighborhood, mothers didn't work out of the home. The smell of cookies baking, or hot raised donuts greeted us every day when we came home from school.

We lived in South Phoenix in the 40s. Street car tracks ran down the center of Washington Street, the main drag. There were two or three theaters on Washington Street. One was the Rialto. It was the cheapest, yet it was elegant, with thick crimson velvet curtains framing the screen and hundreds of tiny lights twinkled in the ceiling.

With the main lights off, it was like sitting outside on a lawn on a starry night. The sound of the streetcar rumbling by barely made a noise through the thick walls.

My sister liked cowboy movies and I loved musicals so we took turns each week. As young as she was, I think she was smarter. She liked cliffhangers, where we had to come back the next week to see how they ended. Naturally my musical choice was postponed a week and she sneaked an extra movie in on me. I never caught on until now that I'm writing this. Talk about a slow learner!

We carefully selected our treat; having to save money for bus fare home. I adored those little hard candy-coated licorice pieces. Donna usually chose Ju-Ju Bs and then tried to whisper with her teeth stuck together. Sometimes when something sad happened she began sniffling and I had to find a hanky for her, making fun of her while wiping my own eyes with the back of my hand. As older sister, it was my job to be cool.

Saturday afternoons our parents loved to dance and have a few beers in a little local tavern on Washington Street where all the cars parked diagonally, facing into the sidewalk. They left us in the car in front of Newberry's Five and Dime, where all "the action" took place on a lazy Saturday afternoon.

We entertained ourselves by watching passersby, making up outrageous, sad or funny stories about the lives of the strangers based on their expressions, their dress, and their carriage. Even at this early age, I planned to be a writer. At frequent intervals Mother or Daddy brought us out packages of Fritos and soft drinks. Sometimes before they went inside the tavern we went into Newberry's and bought bags of warm popcorn.

I should remember Newberry's well, because I started and ended my juvenile crime spree in that very place. I hungered for a bottle of nail polish for as long as I could remember, but we weren't allowed to buy anything like that. It wasn't a case of religious fervor on our parents' part as much as an ingrained moral notion that kids were supposed to be kids as long as they could, and lipstick and nail polish on girls under sixteen was not a good thing.

I filched the bottle and took it home, hiding it in my dresser drawer. In those days mothers knew exactly what their children owned and didn't own and when she found the nail polish, she confronted me. I broke under the first minute of questioning. Lucky for me I never considered the life of a spy. Besides, I knew my sister would tell on me and then my punishment would be worse. My little sister had to be the world's worst tattletale. It gave her such pleasure that Mother was even annoyed at times. To this day, bless her heart, Donna has a hard time keeping secrets. That's because she got her early practice on me.

Mother escorted me back to Newberry's and called for the manager. There in front of everyone, and I was certain the entire city of Phoenix was on hand to witness my humiliation. I apologized and handed the bottle back. I will always bless the store manager for giving me a stern lecture on shoplifting and what could happen if I embarked on such a foolhardy life of crime. I was never tempted again.

Many years later we moved out onto the desert north of Phoenix, a little area known as Sunnyslope. We lived away from the town, in a house nestled up to a mountain, and mountains surrounded us. It was a charmed existence.

After school, when my few chores were finished, I climbed up to the top of the hill or small mountain behind our house with pen and tablet to write poetry and view the world below me.

Spread out before me were enormous squares of colors—golds, greens, browns. Within the closer patches I saw long, straight rows of growing plants. The fields were a living, breathing, patchwork quilt, spread out at my feet.

On Saturday afternoons my sister and I walked to town to the movies. The movies were run in the local community center on a home-type projector. It was often late dusk when we got out and headed toward home. We had a small yellow plastic flashlight in the shape of Pluto, the dog from Walt Disney. You pushed his tail to turn it on.

Imagine two towheaded girls walking across the desert alone. We didn't have brains enough to be scared—unless the movie had been a Boris Karloff or a vampire movie, then we saw threatening shadows skulking behind every rock and bush.

But I had a secret weapon, my very own Guardian Angel. If Donna ever claimed one, I don't know to this day.

There were probably rattlesnakes all around in the cool night desert, not to mention scorpions and uncovered mine shafts too, but we never looked for them and never saw them. Once we heard a noise behind us on a mountain, rocks rolling down. We beamed our puny flashlight and fancied we saw eyes glowing in the dark. The next Saturday night on the trail, we heard the same noise. We waited quietly and saw what appeared to be a huge black cat racing down the mountain, we were certain, toward us. We ran most of the way home.

When we told our parents, they smiled, knowing how wild our imaginations could be. Several months later someone shot a panther said to have traveled down from the mountains of Flagstaff.

The desert was really a neat place to live when you are a kid. The roof of our house was flat with about a foot of a rim around the edges. Donna and I slept up there some hot summer nights, first sweeping the scorpions away. One night we took our rollaway cots out onto the front lawn and thought we'd sleep there, but only once. It was weird to wake up in the middle of the night and hear snorting and snuffling noises. We saw Javalina pigs roaming around the yard. They ignored our presence, and we pulled the sheets up over our heads and tried to ignore them.

Donna could come up with some doozies of ideas too. Once we saw a young rattler sunning itself in the middle of the dirt road in front of our house. She thought we needed to skin it and surprise our father with a snakeskin belt. I managed to hold the head down with a towel and she took a kitchen knife to get her belt. We figured the snakes shed their skin anyway so it was not going to hurt it. Needless to say the snake squirmed away unharmed but probably very indignant and we didn't get our snakeskin belt.

When I began dating at the prescribed age of sixteen, my sister had to come with us as a chaperone at first. That was real cozy. I had one boyfriend who used to give her a quarter if she would disappear temporarily and give us a few minutes alone. In those days we called it "necking", a little hugging, a little kissing—everything above the neck, that was what necking meant.

#

A lot of years have gone by since those days. My sister and I still have traits that annoy each other. We are opposites in many ways. She likes country-western music, I like jazz. She dotes on NASCAR and I enjoy watching figure skating. I read metaphysical books and every self-help book that comes out and she loves historical romances. She has an accountant brain while I am math-a-phobic. Yet she doesn't like to write a letter while I've penned many novels. She's a Republican and I'm a Democrat and we *never* discuss politics. We even put the bathroom tissue and paper towels on the opposite way.

I wish all sisters might find each other and revel in their differences, share the joy, support and love that comes from having a sister who's also a best friend.

TO MY SISTER, DONNA

Sometimes life just goes on by until we think a minute

of those whose presence bless our lives just being in it.

A sister is a lovely word and friend is sometimes better

But put them both together it describes you to the letter.

I love you for your caring, your kind and generous ways

a shoulder there to cry on—we've shared sad and happy days.

You always have believed in me, even when I despaired

of ever being a writer—you supported and you cared.

I guess what I'm trying hard to say is don't give up on me.

When I don't show I love you it should be very plain to see.

We share a bond of friendship that sticks like Crazy Glue.

I know you're always there for me and I'll be there for you.

6.

SPECIAL RECIPES

No book about my thoughts would be complete without offering a handful of my favorite, most unusual recipes. I have always looked upon cooking and baking as a creative process. Oh, sometimes I just throw something together to get a meal out of the way, but through the years, starting as a girl who couldn't boil water, my culinary skills eventually made me proud. I remember the first pie I baked as a newlywed. Bringing the lovely blueberry pie from the oven, I dropped it face down on the kitchen floor. It was quite a while later when I baked another pie, a cherry pie, forgetting to take out the pits.

My improvement in the kitchen evolved through trials, errors and listening to older and wiser women who were glad to share their knowledge with me.

Fall on the farm brings back memories of crisp, cold mornings, leaves beginning to turn on the trees and putting away food for the winter.

It was an exciting time, with the hustle bustle of everyone working at top speed, trying to beat the first snow. The tangy sweet smell of apples ripening in baskets filled the air. They were the bruised ones, to be used for cider making.

But it was a sad time too. I am thankful to this day that none of the adults permitted us to watch, but the sound of pig sticking, as they called it, and the squeals of fear and pain of the animals echoed in my ears for a long time.

At my grandparent's farm, a big black bottomed tub filled with fat and rinds was placed over a fire on the ground. The fat would be rendered for lard to make pie crusts, big, fluffy biscuits and for frying raised donuts. Then the pieces of rind were crisped up in the same tub over the fire. My grandfather used to say nothing went wasted on a pig but the squeal.

We kids thought all families set a table with tall, flaky buttermilk biscuits, fresh eggs over easy, strong coffee, real milk with cream on top, thick buttermilk, golden butter, churned by hand on the old wooden churn, and fruit pies with crusts so golden crisp you had to eat every bite.

A partially buried root cellar held shelves with row on row of quart jars of canned peaches, apples, everything Grandma could get her busy fingers on. It was a beauty to behold and sometimes I went down into the cellar to sit and inhale the cool mustiness and look at the splendid jewel-like bounty in that little room.

Just outside the wood plank door, nestled in among the cool grasses, stood a huge ceramic crock with sauerkraut working. I loved to dip my fingers in--to taste that cold, sharp tang in the back of my throat. Huge stalks of rhubarb grew outside the little cellar and we could break off pieces and chew it like candy. Grandpa didn't like that much. He wanted to save the rhubarb for his favorite rhubarb pies.

I often wonder about how these farm people managed to live to a ripe old age, most of them in their late 80's before they succumbed to death. And then they just seemed to wear out, they didn't get Alzheimer's or cancer or the diseases that plague us today. They thrived on everything we are told now we shouldn't eat.

Freshly made scrapple was one of our favorites. Sometimes we had it for supper instead of breakfast, it was so good. Grandmother had this old recipe that is as easy as using a cake mix and it is delicious.

EASY SAUSAGE SCRAPPLE

1 Cup plain cornmeal (yellow or white)
1 teaspoon salt
Dash pepper
1 Cup cold water
3 cups boiling water
1/2 pound pork sausage, cooked, drained and crumbled
2 teaspoon. shredded green onion (optional)

Bring the 3 cups of water to a rolling boil. Combine cornmeal, salt, pepper and cold water in a bowl. Slowly pour into the pot of boiling water, stirring constantly.

Cook until thickened.

Cover and continue cooking over low heat about 5 minutes, stirring occasionally.

Add drained pork sausage and onion, mix well. Pour into an 8 1/2 x 4 1/2 x 2 1/2 loaf pan which has been rinsed in cold water. Cool slightly. Cover and refrigerate overnight.

To serve, cut into 1/2" slices and fry in lightly buttered pan until brown, about 10 minutes per side. Serve hot with syrup. You'll love it!

Recipes have their own charm. The following are two favorites; simple, summery fruit recipes.

Speaking of hot weather, in Yuma, Arizona, we try to maintain a "cooler" reputation, but all the same, summers are hot. How hot is it? We have a breed of lizard only found in the Sonora Desert called a Stick Lizard. The creature carries a little stick under it when it walks in the summer and stops occasionally to stand on the stick to cool its feet. (Or so I've heard)

EASY FRUIT FLUFF

1 16 oz container cottage cheese
1 8 oz can crushed pineapple
1 8 oz container of Cool Whip
1 large package of Jell-O, any flavor you choose
(Either sweetened with sugar or sugar free.)

Add the DRY Jell-O to all the rest of the ingredients and fold in and lightly beat until blended. Pour into a bowl and refrigerate for a couple of hours until the flavors blend.

***

THIS is my very favorite summer fruit recipe. Don't change a thing. It's very important to use these exact ingredients.

GLAZED FRUIT

16 oz. can pineapple chunks
16 oz can apricots
Can Mandarin oranges
small pack of instant vanilla pudding
1 sliced bananas
Maraschino cherries

Drain fruit, setting juice aside. To 1 cup of mixed fruit juice add the instant pudding. Mix and toss gently with fruit to cover well so bananas don't brown.

Great for taking to potlucks with a few sprigs of mint on top, everyone will rave over it.

A FEW WORDS ABOUT BEANS

Beans are a simple food. They come in all shapes, sizes and colors. They have sustained us through the Great Depression, through drought and hunger and all of the problems we Americans hide beneath our collective consciousness, supposing that we are a rich nation, that everyone has a sufficiency. Beans are found in every culture, crossing lines of race and religion. Everyone loves beans.

Here are two recipes that came from the farmland of Wisconsin when Grandma cooked on a cast iron stove.

Once during an electrical storm, lightning zigged through an open kitchen window, zapped across the room and into one open circle of fire and up the stove pipe, blowing the flimsy metal apart in the process. I remember Grandpa looking up from his Bible reading at the kitchen table and remarking, "Ma, I told you them beans was pretty darn powerful."

GRANDMA'S CALICO BEAN SOUP

Put beans in colander and check for stones and floaters. Rise well. Cover with water in a large pot and soak overnight. Or you can bring to a boil and let bubble for two minutes, turn off burner and leave covered for awhile. Accomplishes the same end.

A lot of new recipes call for the cook to drain the beans at this point. Grandma wouldn't have allowed that, claiming all the "good stuff" would go down the drain. Place the beans in a large kettle with cold water to cover. Keep an eye on them; you may have to add a little water as you go along. You don't want the soup too watery, but thick and rich. Simmer, partially covered until beans are tender.

Stir in 1 teaspoon garlic powder or a good, hefty chunk of garlic clove, minced. (Hint: Smash a garlic clove on your drain board or cutting board with the side of a cup or something equally heavy and the skin will peel off easily.) Add one tablespoon dried parsley, 2 teaspoons mixed Italian seasoning, a smidgen of black pepper, and a packet of dried onion and mushroom soup. Salt to taste.

You may not need more salt because of the dried soup mix. Lightly brown a couple of chopped onions, a little diced celery, diced carrots, in a small amount of oil. Add a can of tomato pulp or canned tomatoes mashed up. Grandma used to let us "do" the tomatoes. They were fresh from the garden and when she turned her back, we—with clean hands, of course—squished them through our fingers to get them just right. Then we had to hurry and wash the tomato seeds off the stove and the wall. I've always wondered if she puzzled why we wanted to do that particular job.

Add 2 cups cooked elbow macaroni and simmer 1/2 hour longer. Grandma wouldn't have sat still for it, but now a cup of wine and Parmesan cheese sprinkled on top caps it off for us.

CALICO BEAN CHEESE BREAD

Cook enough Calico Beans to make 2 cups mashed beans. In a bowl, put 2 cups scalded milk, cooled to lukewarm, with 2 packages of dry yeast. Add the cooked and mashed Calico Beans, 2 teaspoon salt, 2 tablespoons Crisco. (Butter Crisco tastes best.) Stir in 5 to 6 cups flour. Grate 2 cups cheddar cheese

Add enough flour for a workable dough. Turn onto a floured board and knead in cheese. Knead dough about 10 minutes. This is an excellent time to get your day's frustrations out.

Place in a greased bowl, grease top and cover. Let rise in a warm place about 1 hour, until doubled. Punch down, cover and let rise again to double. Divide dough into 6 balls of fairly equal size. Set 3 aside and take 1 ball and roll between your hands forming a long, narrow stick. Do the same with the other two balls. Then lay the 3 sticks on top of each other at one end. Mash tight so they hold and braid the 3 together. Repeat with the other 3 balls and put on a greased cookie sheet, large enough to allow expansion room. Cover and let rise until double. Brush with beaten egg or, for a crisp crust, brush with ice water. Sprinkle top with sesame or poppy seeds. Bake at 350 for 35 minutes, but don't over bake.

Here are two recipes that are super for company dishes or pot lucks.

POTATO CASSEROLE

1 large bag frozen hash brown potatoes
1 medium chopped onion
1 can cream of potato soup
1 can cream of celery soup
1 carton (12 oz) sour cream
1 Cup crumbled Ritz Crackers
1 stick margarine, melted

Grease a 9 x 13 pan. Mix onion, soups and sour cream. Lightly stir into frozen potatoes. Crumble Ritz Crackers to equal 1 cup and sprinkle over potatoes. Melt 1 stick margarine and drizzle potatoes and crackers. Bake at 300 degrees for 1 1/2 hours.

You can vary the soups, cream of broccoli and cheese soups are good to exchange. Serves 6.

***

GREEN RICE

1 cup dry Minute Rice
1 box frozen chopped broccoli
3/4 cup chopped onion
3/4 cup chopped celery
1 can cream of chicken soup
1 can cream of mushroom soup
Grated cheese for topping.
Grease a medium size square or round casserole dish. Mix ingredients together well except for cheese. Bake 30 minutes at 350 degrees. Remove from oven and cover with Cheese   Pop back in the oven until cheese melts.

Toward the end of his life when he couldn't see or hear much, Pappy didn't cook, but before that, he was always self-sufficient. He shared these two special recipes with me. They are easy to make and good eating even if you aren't a 'bo.

HOBO BREAD

#1   Mix: 2 cups raisins
2 cups boiling water
1 1/2 teaspoon soda

Cover and leave overnight.

#2   Next day:

Turn oven to 350 degrees
.

Mix 2 cups sugar
4 cups flour
1 teaspoon cinnamon
1 teaspoon salt
1/4 cup oil

Optional: chopped nuts

Mix 2nd part and combine with 1st part. It will be hard to mix, okay to leave a little lumpy (like a hobo's bedroll). Grease and flour 2 bread pans. Hoboes traditionally made this in 1# coffee cans. Bake 1 hour and 15 minutes at 350 degrees. Watch so it doesn't brown too much.

This is Pappy's other recipe. I don't know where this bread recipe got its name.

Maybe the 'bo's were rubbing it in that they had an easy, wonderful bread and the housewives didn't have the recipe. Now you do.

HA HA BREAD

Turn on oven at 350 degrees.

Combine 3 cups self rising flour
3 Tablespoons sugar
1/4 teaspoon salt
1 can of beer (flat or not, doesn't matter)

Mix ingredients and pour in greased loaf or coffee can.

Bake 1 hour.

NO BAKE CHOCOLATE COOKIES

Put in pan and bring to a boil:

2 Cups sugar	1/2 teaspoon salt
1/2 Cup milk	2 Tablespoons cocoa

1/4 Cup butter or margarine (not whipped type)

Cook 1 minute. Add 1/2 cup peanut butter. Stir until smooth.

Remove from heat and quickly add 1 teaspoon vanilla and 3 cups of quick oats.

Stir well. Nuts optional. Pour into buttered 9x13x2 pan. Cool before cutting.

DELICIOUS NUT CAKES

2 cups sifted cake flour	1 cup sugar
2 teaspoons baking powder	1 egg
1 cup chopped walnut pieces	1/4 tsp salt
4 Tablespoons shortening	¾ Cup milk

1 teaspoon vanilla extract

Sift flour and baking powder together. Cream the shortening thoroughly, add sugar gradually, continuing to cream until light and fluffy. Add egg and beat thoroughly. Add nuts. Stir in dry ingredients, a small amount at a time, alternately with milk, to which vanilla extract has been added. Baat after each addition until smooth. Pour into greased square pan (8 x 8 x 2), and bake in moderate oven (350 degrees) for 50 minutes. Or bake in a greased loaf pan (8 x 4 1/2 x 3 1/2) for about the same time, testing with toothpick in center. I like to use miniature cake forms, wrap individually in clear plastic wrap and give for Christmas. This is a truly delicious, delicate cake that will become a family favorite.

LEMON WHIPPERSNAPPERS

1 egg
1 teaspoon lemon extract
1 package lemon cake mix
2 cups whipped topping (such as Cool whip)

Beat one egg and 1 teaspoon lemon extract together.

Sift 1 lemon cake mix and add with 2 cups whipped topping.

Drop by teaspoon on a baking sheet and bake until golden.

***

SALMON CASSEROLE

For this surprisingly simple but great tasting dish, you need about 44 Cheeze-It type crackers, 2 cups milk and a can of salmon and about 1/4 cup grated cheese.

Pulverize cheeze crackers, and cook with milk until it is the consistency of white sauce. Open a can of salmon; mash it up with the juice so it's all blended together. Cover the bottom of a greased casserole dish with a layer of this salmon. Spread part of the sauce on top, then another layer of salmon, etc until you finish with the sauce on top. Sprinkle grated cheese on top. Bake at 350 degrees until bubbly.

You can always substitute Tuna for the salmon.

***

Another salmon recipe is for puffy patties. Easy.

SALMON PUFFY PATTIES

1 egg
1 can salmon and juice
1 teaspoon Worcestershire sauce
1 teaspoon oil
garlic powder to taste
flavored salt to taste
cheese crackers crumbled very fine (in blender).

Mix first 5 ingredients. Add enough crumbled crackers to salmon mix so it will hold together when you pat out cakes about 1/4" thick and as big as your palm. They don't have to be exactly the same, of course. Sauté both sides lightly in a little hot oil until nice and brown.

At the risk of angering someone over an endangered species, the last recipe I want to share is this delicious recipe for:

ELEPHANT STEW.

1 medium elephant
2 rabbits (optional)
Salted and peppered brown gravy.

Cut the elephant into bite-sized pieces. This should take about two months.

Add enough brown gravy to cover. Cook over kerosene fire for about four weeks at 465 degrees.

This will serve 3,500 people. If more are expected, two rabbits may be added, but do this only if necessary, as some people do not like to find a hare in their stew.

EXCUSES—EXCUSES

I used to bake goodies, so perfect & fine.

Every morsel delicious, I was proud it was mine.

But as I grew older, I must tell the truth,

My baking skills seemed to stay back in my youth.

I may leave an egg out or add too much butter,

Put in chips but not nuts, oh my what a clutter.

So cut me some slack and in case you don't know it,

You have my permission to go on and throw it.

With good, yummy recipes I felt obligated to share my diet and exercise tips.

DIET TIPS

1) Calories disappear into the atmosphere as ice cream melts.

2) If you eat while reading or watching TV, the calories

   don't add up because you don't see them.

3) Calories evaporate into steam when you taste food while

   cooking.

4) If you don't eat some fat daily, such as well marbled

   steaks, your skin dries and wrinkles.

5) If a candy bar is frozen only half the calories count,

   since it uses twice as many calories to chew it.

6) The more coffee you drink with a Danish, the more

   calories you wash away.

7) When you eat standing at the kitchen sink where no one

   can see you, calories count less.

8) If you exercise daily you will end up with a VERY

   healthy appetite and unsightly muscles.

9) If you leave food on your plate to show off at a family gathering, the

food you sneak later will not be fattening, due to the time element.

10) Leftovers have few calories. They are mostly dried out by the time
you eat them.

YOU KNOW YOU NEED AEROBICS WHEN. . .

It takes 15 minutes to pull up your Leotards

You decide you need a governor on your Exercycle

You try a pushup and can't get your nose out of the carpet

You get short of breath whipping potatoes—and you're using a blender

You bend down to touch your toes and can't find them

You buy panty hose in Queen Size and can't pull the crotch above your thighs

YOU KNOW YOU NEED AEROBICS WHEN. . .

You push an empty cart all over the grocery store just for support

You really aren't hungry--but you eat every left over on the table

Your designer jeans are by Roseanne

Your thighs rub together and your pants catch on fire

Your stomach and bust measurements are equal

THAT'S WHEN YOU KNOW—YOU NEED AEROBICS!

7.

NATURE

DANCE OF A SUNFLOWER

Last night I witnessed the midnight dance of a Sunflower.

A wild sunflower, about fifteen feet tall, its head

the size of a dinner plate, grew on an empty lot next door.

Small blossoms sprouted from all angles on the main stalk,

spreading out with little stems at the bottom like a colorful print skirt.

A light breeze blew gently through the fronds of the sunflower

branches while a full moon shone down with a pale, silent smile.

BIRDS FLY OVER MARSHLANDS

In the east, birds fly low over marshlands

while the bold light of day

spreads crystal traces of rose upon their wings.

Westward, the full moon hangs above the cloud line

as if reluctant to sink below the horizon

and relinquish the night.

Distant shadows veil purple mountains

with a soft infusion of haze.

The desert floor prepares for the new day.

Something there is about a flower...

Something there is about flowers that despise constriction. My yard blooms with reckless abandon. Plants grow willy-nilly, colors clashing in loving freedom.

My neighbor insists on strict order and discipline in his plants. In return, he begets joyless, abject displays of greenery, interspersed with faint colors deep inside his hedges, as if ashamed to be seen. Is life like a garden, I wonder? Does beauty beg to be free? When we put our life in order, compartmentalize, segregate, divide, plan, decree—does it spoil the blooms of life?

I feel sorry for people who must always have control, who insist that everyone and everything correspond with their private sense of order.

Admittedly, some control is necessary in a garden. Weeds cannot be allowed to intrude. Aphids, snails and caterpillars cannot be permitted to roam freely. We abide by natural rules of order like watering, fertilizing, picking dead blooms, and setting out new plants. All this requires a bit of control, but I like to keep it as non-invasive as possible. My garden knows pretty well what to do without a lot of help from me.

I let my garden bloom itself into a frenzy of disordered beauty. The same way I try to allow my thoughts to go uncensored and unrestrained, to exercise a diminishing control so that I harbor few expectations. My flowers can do as they please and my friends are not required to think as I do, or behave in my image. It may be the best way to tend to a garden, to nurture life and it will allow me to unfold and continue to bloom in my own time and way.

New Day's Dawn

I saw a slash of dawn today

as a narrow white cloud ripped diagonally

across the sky,

tearing apart the satiny peach blush

of the slowly rising sun.

Smoothly, the soft backgrounds

ebbed and flowed

around and into the intrusive cloud until

it was no more.

Unobstructed, the sun crept up,

creating its soft, serene dawn.

Lessons surround us in nature

one needs only to observe

that which slashes and tears apart

the fabric of our lives.

With gentle pressure of non acceptance

we can regain our harmony:

the tranquility we need

to start each dawning day.

No Vegetables Allowed

My garden's filled with roses

and creeping, unruly flowers.

It's total anarchy, none are submissive

The petunias are apt to tower.

The ground cover grows in ridges,

eschewing the bottom line.

While the jasmine creeps and crawls

Oblivious to an upward climb.

Friends ask if I've planted tomatoes

They grow squash and lettuce galore

My flowers would be devastated

To share space with mundane bores.

So I smile and say no to the carrots

and frown when it comes to bok choy.

In my garden there lives not one practical thing

except for colorful riotous joy.

I wrote this when I was 13, so I keep it as a reminder of my early thoughts.

GOD'S SYMPHONY

Mountains of gray, skies of blue,

Flowers so bright, clean shiny dew.

Stars from the sky, soft moon above

Tell the sweet story, of God's true love.

Pink sun is setting, deep in the west,

Painting a portrait of serenity's best.

High in the cactus, soft breezes blow,

This is God's love song, He made it so.

A symphony, God's Symphony...

A song of praise from sky to sea.

He made it all—a perfect bliss,

A symphony—His tender kiss.

All things you see, made by God's hand

Are miracles that He has planned.

Whisper of winds, sounds of the seas...

All are a part of—God's Symphony.

PAINTING A DESERT CANVAS

Golden brown stubble, color of Viking's beard

twisted and sharded fields of cut hay mellowing in

the daybreak haze.

In the distance purple mountains sprawl, shrouded

by wisps of puffy clouds as flocks of white birds,

wings traced with rose,

soar across the horizon, melting into the penumbra of dawn.

Burnished sunrise brushes a rainbowed sweep

across a sapphire sky with a hint of moisture in the air—

promise of life to the thirsty earth waiting below

as the desert awakes.

SUMMER IN YUMA

We're card carrying members
of an elite group from hell.
August in Yuma
will bear that out well.

The devil vacations
just south of Bard,
his own private playground,
and Yuma's back yard.

Sometimes in hell,
when the burners get low,
the flames all die down
and the heat fails to glow

Then he comes to Yuma--
most times on the sly.
To charge up his energy
on our July.

And when he goes home,
he giggles and gloats, but
until he gets seasoned,
he must wear his coat.

Later hell heats up
when Yuma turns cool.
but in thinking this over,
we're playing the fools.

Why don't we all take our
summers in hell?
Let the devil take Yuma
—we'll get even as well.

PHOTOGRAPHS NOT TAKEN

Quite often I see things and wish for a camera. Too often I have had a camera handy, taken the picture, and was disappointed because it looked nothing like my mind's picture. Or I stuck the photo in a box.

Over the years I have accumulated a photograph album of word pictures. Study the interesting scene; let your mind hear the words, listen to a description of the picture in the back of your eyes and not through the front. You can do it, too. When you see a sunrise that moves you, when you see a baby's toothless grin as he's carried through a crowd, when you see a flower too beautiful to describe, take a moment, grab a pen and scrap of paper and make a word picture.

You don't have to be a writer, only an observer. You'll be surprised at what you notice. Or better yet, keep a journal of "photographs not taken". Photographs that you will remember long after those thrown in a box that you intend to put in albums on a rainy day.

NEW YORK STATE:

. . . Lightening bugs, solid across the meadow, threading in and out through a wispy fog, a red-winged black bird soaring across a green field —sun sparkling on its wings.

. . . A bay horse standing, munching grass in a field of yellow buttercups.

. . . Fog drifting in from the lake at dusk. The full moon begins to penetrate—eerily sifting the fog through molten moonbeams. As the wind blows, the fog scuds across the lake in little cotton candy puffs.

. . . Small deer poised, listening, on the brink of crossing the road--then springing lightly up the bank of a bright green slope covered with daisies.

. . . Patches of green alfalfa interspersed with tan fields of freshly cut hay. Precise little squares lying around scattered like dominoes.

. . . Glistening, gold/brown stubble of new mown hay. Cut wheat bristling in early morning sun like a Viking's beard. Three empty wooden wagons stand vigil over the ravaged field.

. . . Rose-red sun swimming through a mackerel sky filled with puffy pink clouds.

. . . Riding down a twisty country road. Early morning sun up, still hazy from light fog. Meadow grasses covered with dew make solid fields look like sparkling shards of glass. Black and white cows grazing, serenely at peace. Silence reigns, except for the occasional trill of a meadowlark or a red winged blackbird.

***

PENNSYLVANIA

. . . Fog creeping noiselessly through apple trees in crisp autumn morning. Crackly crunchy leaves, sighing, sifting gently to the soft, dew-covered ground. Gold, orange, red--like multicolored rainbow fragments falling from a giant's jewelry box. A king's ransom in beauty.

. . . Small village--pastel colored houses. Steep roofs nestled snugly in a valley surrounded by trees dressed in fall colors.

. . . Girl in red slacks, piling bright orange pumpkins in a leaf strewn yard. Black and white kitten tumbling in the leaves.

. . A rain of rainbow leaves. Wind blowing, leaves falling in a splendid profusion of colors. Sun sifting down on tree lined road, bold, green, pale red, orange, leaves twisting and turning in the breeze, silver shimmering on the backs as they twirl.

***

OKLAHOMA

. . . Long red road leading to a white fenced farm house. Smoke from chimney in the early evening haze.

. . . Still pond—tree ringed reflections skirting the edges, rippling with insects or surfacing fish.

. . . Shiny, eye -hurting red clay. Miles and miles of plowed earth. Where are the trees?

. . . Spindly legged colt, nuzzling against its mother in early morning dew-encrusted grass.

NEW MEXICO

. . . Red rocks. Odd shaped, strong and delicate, whimsical and serious. Indian woman colorfully dressed entering drab mud-packed home.

. . . Albuquerque—nestling between two mountain ridges. Green fertile fields, snow covering ground, smog encrusting early morning air.

***

TEXAS

. . . Wind. Wind. Wind. Whistling fiercely through telephone wires, RV rocking, vibrating. Dark, ugly clouds peering from behind tall silos. Everything seems poised—waiting for the wind to change.

. . .   Green rolling meadows. Lone immense pine with a carpet of soft purple flowers spread at its base.

. . . Space, an eternity of time to cross Texas.

NATURE

I share my God with Nature.   I have no creed but love.

When I die I need no mourners or Psalms from high above.

There's no need for sorrow, but if you would remember me

when you witness Nature's beauty, wish that I were there to see.

A falling leaf, a bright gold star, a brown and yellow sparrow,

A russet tree, a lake of sun, the river dark and narrow.

Purple mountains, gray-green trees the desert—strong and silent,

Icy snows, lace trimmed pines winter calm and violent.

A dainty, fragile butterfly, a gentle, cooing dove,

I share my God with Nature, I need no creed but love.

Believe it or not, up to this past week, (in June) the weather has been semi-pleasant. I suppose describing summer in Yuma, Arizona as semi-pleasant is like saying one is semi-pregnant. In the summer when the temperature hits in the middle 90s we are having a "cool-down". By the same token, in the winter when the temperature hits 65 we reach for our jackets and electric blankets.

***

When I edited the newsletter for our writing group, I penned these words pertaining to summer:

"Due to circumstances that preclude any predilection on the part of SUNSHINE WRITERS as an organization of multitudinous mendacity, the meeting for the month of July was abrogated, obliterated, terminated due to the paucity of available constituents.

In other words, it was hotter'n haydees and we all stayed home in the shaydees."

***

Seasons are great, don't you agree? Fall has always been my favorite. Living in the desert southwest, I hear visitors complain about our "lack of seasons." Not true! We have lovely seasonal changes, more subtle and graceful than those changes back East, but we definitely have seasons.

Nature is an overworked word, but as a word, it is so powerful, so strong, so thought provoking.

EAST AND WEST

East, with her jaded, overblown beauty—

flaming hair the color of autumn,

Eccentric, overdressed, wearing purple and red.

She drives a three wheeled bike with a motor.

A lady who loves crowds, noise and excitement.

She drenches herself with the perfume of rain,

wears earrings of jagged lightning bolts,

and flashes a deep piled coat of ermine white in winter.

West is a genteel, delicately-aging dowager

with lean, subtle beauty—never tawdry or overdone.

She values privacy, hates showing off. Excess a vulgarity.

As she spreads her long wide skirt in spring,

few notice the tiny purple flowers,

the sparse, fragile blossoms of yellow and gold

entwined with her practical grays and browns.

She never courts praise, content with respect,

'Just enough' is her essence.

AUTUMN RAINS

Crispy, crackly golden leaves

ever falling, drifting, sliding

as the trees sway gracefully,

following the breeze.

On the ground they float—swim—

red, gold, pale yellow, orange.

Still on the trees--their green brothers sigh

—longing to follow.

MORNING

A soft carpet of plush emerald green spreads across the floor of the forest. Early morning dew plays gently upon soft petals of brightly painted flowers. Tall scented pines sway gracefully with each caressing breeze. Nearby a leaping brook tumbles joyfully. High upon a tree, a dove calls to its mate. Two squirrels scold with raucous abandon.

Then the sun rises—in all its glory. Its bright rays search out every shadow, every corner, even the smallest flower. The soft dew sparkles diamond-like on long stemmed grasses until the floor of the forest is like a sparkling, twinkling carpet of stars.

From the highest of the sweet smelling pines to the lowest sliver of dew washed grass—each in its own way spells morning.

EVENING

Quietly, tenderly, Mother Nature began putting her house in order after a long, busy day. Softly, a gentle breeze sang lullabies to the stilled woodland, lulling even risky squirrels to a drowsy quietness.

High in a scented pine tree, a white dove mourned in lonely solitude. Only the creatures of the night stirred, keeping their silent vigil through the falling twilight.

Suddenly, like a veil thrown over the forest, the sun disappeared below the horizon of the trees. The pink rays of the dying sun set the tallest pine branches aglow and fell, glistening, on the silent brook.

Then all was still. Night had come.

8.

PETS WHO HAVE OWNED ME

Like most everyone, I have had the privilege of living with many wonderful pets. When I was a child, our family always had pets—all kinds, from white rats, to red racers (little snakes), hamsters, rabbits, and parakeets.

Often, coming home from school a stray mutt might follow me, after I petted him, of course. Since we normally had at least two dogs of our own, I was allowed to keep the stray only long enough to clean it up and find a home for it.

Obviously we could not keep every dog or cat we saw. Even at a young age I saw the wisdom behind my father's edict and respected it, although sometimes it was hard to give up an animal I'd rescued.

On Easter my sister and I usually received baby chickens or tiny, cuddly rabbits. In those days they colored the baby chickens with food dye, but it didn't seem to hurt them. They were White Leghorns and turned out fine. All roosters, they crowed their heads off when they grew up until we were forced by neighborhood pressure to find homes for them too. We always exacted promises from the new owners that they wouldn't eat them, but at the same time, we knew we had no control over that.

The rabbits, needless to say, multiplied like....well, you know—rabbits. Soon we had so many! Daddy kept building hutches for them in the back and frankly we got kind of bored feeding and watering them and keeping damp gunny sacks over the cages in the heat of the desert summer.

Daddy thought he came on to a solution when he decided we should eat rabbit instead of chicken for Sunday dinner. To our horror, we figured out the switch from chicken to rabbit. The big heaping plate of crispy fried rabbit sat in the center of the table and we wouldn't touch it or fried chicken again, for a long while, afraid we were being tricked.

We found homes for our bunnies eventually and went out of the rabbit business forever.

I adored turtles. In those days Newberry and Woolworth sold turtles in the back of the store. Someone painted the little turtles, too, although I don't think that could have been too comfortable for them. It was a common practice and we never thought to protest. At any rate, Mother bought me quite a few turtles as I was growing up and they usually lived to a ripe old age until something accidental happened to them. For a treat they ate little pieces of raw hamburger and got quite aggressive when it was feeding time, snatching the little pieces of meat from fingers.

My "turtle job" that I gave myself was to rush into every dime store we visited on Saturday afternoon shopping expeditions and make sure the turtles in the rear of each store were all turned right side up. Believe me, I had a few turtles to turn over every time, and worried between Saturdays if they were okay until I got there.

I loved white rats, but they do have a distinctive odor all their own even if they seem immaculate, always cleaning themselves as cats do. I wore my hair in a long pageboy and my white rat nestled against my neck and poked his head out as I took him for "walks" in the afternoons.

Once our father bought a donkey that loved to drink beer or cokes. If you put the bottle in his mouth, he tilted it up and gurgle, gurgle, it was soon gone. He always waited patiently for you to retrieve the bottle from his teeth and he never broke a bottle.

My sister and I had a lot of fun with the donkey. I was taking Spanish in high school and named him Picaro, which meant rascal. We called him Pikky for a while, but that sounded too much like my name, so we finally called him the English version of Rascal.

But it's true about donkeys being stubborn. One lazy summer afternoon we cut across a nearby crop dusting air-field as a short cut and, wouldn't you know, a plane decided to land just then? I think we must have been in the way, or the pilot was having fun with us, because he seemed to be coming right at us. Do you think we could get that silly burro to hurry? We didn't abandon him to his fate, although I think we should have. We stayed with him until the plane passed over our heads.

In later years I had aquariums with lovely fan-tailed gold fish that grew to alarming sizes in a fifteen-gallon container. Part of their growth could have come from feeding them spaghetti (without the sauce, of course). They loved it. Maybe it went back to their ancient memory of eating sea worms.

Over the years I've had many goldfish and each loved spaghetti. The moment I dropped about two inches of pasta, they swam up to grab it. Sometimes they each took an end and met in the middle. Once, before I got into buying aquariums for my goldfish, I kept one in a large fishbowl. During the night, it leaped out onto the carpet. The next morning I found it, barely alive. I ran water over it carefully under the faucet and pressed gently on its little sides, blowing into its mouth. Believe it or not the fish began wriggling and survived the ordeal. Not many people I know have the distinction of giving a fish CPR and I'm not bragging about it.

Sometimes I feel like "Mother Earth" because upon arising each morning, I go outside and feed the wild birds, and check to see if the hummingbird feeders are full. Then the stray cats get their share of dry cat food. Fuzzy-Buzzy, Knobby, Twoie and Harley, my personal cats, need to be fed. My dogs, Daisy and Schnoodles, get to eat after their walk. Then I have breakfast. By then several cheeky road runners come up for their daily meals of raw hamburger. I can always tell when they are nesting because they come in pairs and neither one eats the meat, but pick up two or three pieces in their beaks and take off for their babies.

***

Pets bring such comfort and unconditional love. People who can't spare the time or energy, or just plain don't want a pet, are to be pitied. Scientists have proven that older people live longer when they have a pet.

I should probably live to be 200.

BLACK CAT

My father had several odd habits, especially when he had a few drinks under his belt. I thought his weirdest notion came from the expectation that our dogs should perform circus tricks when, in truth, we never taught them as much as a handshake.

Neither my sister nor I cared a whit if our pets could play dead or roll over, or whatever makes people think teaching pets to perform parlor tricks was entertainment.

To give him credit, Daddy never lost his temper. He always had a puzzled look on his face while the dogs sat in front of him, staring with heads cocked, as if politely wondering what he wanted them to do—and why.

I often thought of teaching my dog Pal to play dead, just to surprise my dad, but changed my mind. Probably Pal would then have been asked to climb ladders or trees or jump through a burning hoop.

From early on, we were taught to respect the feelings of animals and never cause them harm. Once my father suffered burns to his hands by rescuing rabbits from a neighbor's burning shed. But he did set limits. When I was about twelve, a black tom cat turned up at our door. He was never very friendly. He barely tolerated us to touch him, although we were welcome to feed him. He was so distant that we just called him Black Cat instead of trying to come up with an interesting name as we usually did for our pets.

Daddy tended to be superstitious and never liked black cats, but he couldn't say no to us when we asked to let the cat stay.

One thing he was adamant about, drinking or sober. No cat was ever allowed on the table. That was the cardinal sin of all animaldom. Daddy came home one night ,after a few beers at the local tavern, and Black Cat had jumped upon Mother's clean white table cloth where he still sat, nonchalantly cleaning his whiskers. Daddy took a swipe at the cat, expecting the animal to get out of the way, but I guess my father was fast or Black Cat was slow because the cat landed up against the wall and lay very still, crumpled on the floor.

We wailed and carried on; you'd think we liked the dumb cat. I still recall my dad's shamefaced look when he ordered us to stay inside while he buried the cat. He couldn't have buried him very deep because the next evening when he came home from having a few beers at the local tavern, the cat was on the front porch again. Daddy abstained from alcohol for a few weeks after that and Black Cat eventually wound up living at my grandmother's house miles across town.

I guess she wasn't superstitious or maybe none of us told her the whole story of Black Cat.

Home is a Castle

A home is a castle or so someone said.

In my Queendom I'm first in command.

I make rules for my subjects to follow—

and I rule with an iron hand.

My dogs are at home in a fenced yard,

they bark at the drop of a hat.

I forbid them and yell, they look rather shamed,

but bark even louder at that.

My cats roam freely and allow me to buy

food they may actually eat.

They know my rules to come home at dark,

and sometimes they manage that feat.

In obedience training, my dog came in last.

She's gentle and sweet but quite willful.

I open the door when she rings the bells.

Don't you think that's quite skillful?

I'm Queen of the land, in my fenced in yard.

My dominion—love tempered with hassles.

Someday I may outsmart all these critters, who knows?

That's why I'm at home in my castle.

If there is a major flaw or quirk in my thinking, it is my lifetime love for God's creatures. A macho movie star was quoted once as saying," Why not kill a deer? They aren't all Bambis, you know." Or words to that effect. No, they aren't all Bambis, but they once were.

One of my cats brought me a field mouse as a gift. The little mouse was quite dazed so I had time to race to the bathroom, retrieve a wash cloth and scoop it up. I took it out past my yard in the field and let it go. I'm not proud of that, it was just something I had to do.

Although I can slay mosquitoes and flies with reckless abandon, don't ask me to swat a bumble bee. When one finds its way onto a window in the house, I take a glass and a paper and capture it to let it outside. The bird bath in the back yard is sometimes filled with drinking bees. When I put the hose on it to make it fresh, I warn them, "Sting me once, and you won't get another drop of water from me." This has been going on for years and as they swarm around me, they seem to understand and have never stung the hand that watered them. With the new breed of outlaw bees around, though, I'm ready to bolt and run for the back door.

Once a daddy longlegs spider made a comfortable home in the corner of the metal storage shed. Just for kicks, I brought him an occasional dazed fly I swatted and threw it on the web. Over the months the spider grew fat and looked like no daddy longlegs I'd ever seen before. When he saw me coming he vibrated the web in excitement and I gave him dinner. Finally a friend noticed the fat, juicy spider when she came to visit and looked in the shed. That was the end of him. Some people just don't share my enthusiasm for critters.

The other day I noticed big red ants making off with cracked corn that was part of the bird feed I strew in the street in front of my house several times a day. Indignant, I walked out there and saw several ants industriously carrying giant pieces of cracked corn and heading in the same direction. I followed them past my neighbor's house, past a vacant lot, past another lot, until they led me right up to the large mound, which was their home. I watched them enter and then fancied I saw the same workers emerge and head back for another load.

What a fascinating display of diligence to trudge over hot pavement in 110 degree weather, to walk nearly a block and then deposit their burden and turn around to do it over and over. I don't imagine they were even offered a drink of water. Well, as far as I'm concerned they can stay there as long as they want if the dopey birds can't defend their food, who am I to intrude?

LOBO

I once had a long-haired Chihuahua who looked like a tiny lion. In his whole life, he loved only me. This was flattering at first, but it became a little unnerving to guests. As soon as they stood up to leave and got as far as the door, he ran forward and bit their heels. I spanked him with papers, yelled at him, but to no avail. He thought he was protecting me. It got so I had to put him in the bedroom before our guests departed.

I named him Lobo, thinking the name ironic, but it didn't turn out that way. If he had been of any size, he might have been dangerous. Friends and family were quick to point out that if I had been sensible and named him Flower or Sweetie Pie, he might have had a whole different outlook on life. They tried to lay a guilt trip on me. I had programmed my dog to act like a wolf by naming him that.

Lobo had another peculiarity, a doggie obsession. He had a purse fetish. I always set my purse down by my favorite chair. He considered it his job to guard that purse with snarling possessiveness. When guests sat in that chair, they'd better not put a hand down near that purse! It got so bad that when visitors set their handbags down Lobo began his guard job and wouldn't let them pick up their own purses until I distracted him.

In later years Lobo didn't even want me to touch my own purse. I finally wised up. I gave him an old, discarded purse, and he was happy. That's probably what he wanted all along, his own purse to guard. He truly was a special dog, though, and in spite of his bad habits everyone who saw him thought him beautiful. He lived to a ripe old age of fifteen. He died gently during the night and we buried him inside his purse.

TAKE ONE GOPHER A DAY

My husband of thirty-one years loved to garden and always liked to tease me because I not only didn't have a green thumb, it must have been purple. When my husband passed away, I didn't want his garden to die, so I took over.

In a month's time the gophers spread the word about a novice gardener and ran rampant. They had so many holes I didn't have to till the soil, only to wait for them to dig it for me. My two lazy cats watched all this activity, but refused to let it annoy them.

Someone told me to put mothballs down their holes. They kicked them out. A wild castor bean tree grew in a nearby field and I gathered the poisonous beans to throw down the holes. They loved them. For all I know they decorated their dens with them. Every bean disappeared.

When I planted a row of little tomato plants, the next morning the entire row vanished, sucked downward and the evidence covered up as if the plants had never been.

Animal lover that I was, this was too much. I still didn't want to set actual killing traps, but I had one last ally. My dog Schnoodles. I was desperate enough to turn her loose on the rascals. A schnauzer and poodle mix, Schnoodles has been a hunter and a digger from puppyhood. She took on the challenge when I pointed out the holes, sitting and waiting for hours to see beady little eyes appear. She'd cock her head as if she heard the gophers underneath the grass. Unfortunately she dug more holes than the gophers, and not nearly as neatly. They had to have known she was there, seldom returning to the original hole, but merely digging another.

I blamed every gardening woe on the gophers. A tree expired and I figured they'd gotten to the roots. A rose bush took a turn for the worse, I know now it was moldy fungus, but the gophers got blamed for that. Actually, I should have left the gophers alone, they were good as scapegoats and I didn't figure to enjoy gardening anyway.

One afternoon as I sat outdoors relaxing in the peace and quiet, something a garden is actually good for, I noticed what looked like a small cord hanging from Schnoodles' mouth. The dog didn't seem to be in distress, but I could tell she was nervous. I called her to me and started pulling gently on the string.

As I tugged on it, she held perfectly still, and here came the rear end, the middle and then the head of a gopher. It was dazed, but still alive. The only thing I could figure is that Schnoodles sat in the sun, panting with her mouth open, waiting at a gopher hole. The little critter must have launched itself out of the hole right into her waiting mouth. She didn't bite down; she was afraid to swallow, and came looking for me.

Schnoodles was ecstatic to have the operation over and licked my hand joyfully. I tossed the confused gopher over the fence into the vacant lot, hoping he'd appreciate his luck and leave me alone in the future.

After that, the gophers must have passed the word around about the determined gardener. Schnoodles didn't dig in the back yard for months and the slight tingle of the wind chimes may have been my husband, smiling.

DAISY

Daisy is about the sweetest dog, with the most endearing personality that I've ever known. She has one major flaw. She is stubborn to the max. Being half springer spaniel and half terrier, both breeds energetic, I thought it would be best to enter her in a dog training session. The first time in my life I'd ever done such a thing.

There were twelve dogs in the class besides Daisy. German Shepards, mixed labs, a Sharpei, all big dogs. Each and every dog trotted around, sitting and staying and slavishly obeying all of the commands as if their lives depended upon it.

All but one dog. Daisy. At first the instructor blamed me. She said I wasn't handling her properly. When Daisy wouldn't obey her either, she graciously conceded it may not have been my fault. Daisy never raised her voice to a growl or otherwise displayed irritation at being yanked all about the place. She just wouldn't participate.

This was not only humiliating, but made me angry, since I knew Daisy was as smart as or smarter than some of those dogs. I wanted so badly to quit while I still had some dignity, but my husband said, "No, once you start something you see it through." Easy for him to say, he was video taping all of our foolishness to show the neighbors later.

Finally the day of graduation dawned. Daisy came in last, needless to say, but she did get her diploma for $49. Several days later when I took her for a walk, she heeled perfectly without a leash and sat when I asked her to.

I learned a valuable lesson. Not everyone wants or needs to go to school and a person should never try to show off at the expense of a good buddy.

Sunny

You died.
I put you in my garden—sweetest, finest cat
I ever belonged to.

Soft blond kitten,
you engaged me with your gentleness,
charmed me with your tranquil affection.
A tomcat you never were.

The birds—the unharmed birds you brought me
and then waited...
yellow-eyed for my approval.
With regret tinged with laughter,
I beheld your astonished outrage,
long whiskers bristling with your need
to cry out the disappointment
when I let them fly away.

Again and again you tried your trust in me,
and yet I could not help but break it,
to go against my instincts....nor could you.

Sunny Boy, soft golden one.
You lie beneath a mound of yellow flowers,
roots burrowing into your essence and
turning back their beauty
to shame my selfish tears.
The flowers mock me with their strength and purity
as if they say...
he is here...he belongs to us.

THE BIRDS

When I was younger, I lived for a few years in the South. There I was known to many as the Bird Woman. Any spring I knew someone would invariably bring me a baby bird that had fallen from the nest.

Most of them were salvageable, and I could eventually return to the open sky to fly away. I had swallows, sparrows, mocking birds, a sea gull with a broken wing, and a starling. The sparrow was a mite of a bird, no feathers, and ugly as sin. I forgot what I had named him/her, but we bonded and I believe it saw me as Mother Bird. He, (lets not be tedious and do the he/her business,) if they are dumb enough to fall out of the nest they must be male. Anyway, I could go outdoors or even shopping in our little community with him along comfortably perched on my shoulder. The newspaper sent a reporter out to take our pictures. I wanted him to go back to the wild and one spring morning he heard the cry of a lovely female sparrow and vanished into the trees.

My favorite bird though, was Pesky the starling. I found her in the back yard, fallen from the nest and no feathers to speak of. Birds are really very icky looking at that stage, since you can see through their thin skin into the veins and what not but that never bothered me. She became a beautiful bird with speckled brown feathers and quite large. And she really lived up to her name. She sat on my shoulder at meal times and if she saw something really appealing she dashed down and grabbed it off my fork or my plate. She would "kiss" me by opening my lips with her beak. I think my pearly teeth fascinated her.

Once I was canning sweet pickles and she fell into the vat of pickle juice, luckily it wasn't hot, and I had to throw it out and start over plus hold her under the faucet to wash her off. She seemed to love water and we had to keep the toilet seat down or she was prone to dive in and then squawk like the dickens when she couldn't get out.

I started her off with canned dog food, a solid type called Skippy's, I think. I wrote the company about her liking it so much they sent me a couple of cases. This lasted a while. She also loved coffee and she had her own cup with some cream and a little sugar in the morning. Once my husband and I took a trip a little over a hundred miles away to visit some of his kinfolks. We took Pesky in her cage because we couldn't leave her alone for a week. She was happy with the visit and mostly stayed outdoors in the thick trees and flew down to the screen when she wanted in. When we were ready to go one morning, we couldn't find her. We called and looked up in the trees and all over the house to no avail. I felt sad but figured she finally decided she should be a bird.

Several days after we got home the bus company called us to say they had her in a cage and would we come get her. She came back to the house looking for us and wouldn't leave so the folks put her back in the cage and sent her to us. A few years later, she finally heard the call of the wild and gradually stayed away longer and longer until she left the nest finally.

But that wasn't the end of my bird mothering. Just last spring the neighbor boys found a featherless baby bird under their palm tree cornered by their dog. They brought it to me and it was so noisy I named it Squeaky. I figured it was either a blackbird or a mocking bird, hard to tell, but it had to be an insect eater. I started it on cat food and it spit it out. Ditto dog food. But it did like raw hamburger so that was the diet combined with jars of fruity baby food once in awhile.

You haven't lived until you put a spoonful of baby food into a bird's beak and have him fling it around the room and over your front if he didn't like it.

At the time I have a sort of cat sanctuary so needless to say I had to keep him in my computer room in a cat cage so none of the felines could catch a glimpse of him. But darn it all, I couldn't shut him up. He made continual bird noises, tweeting and sputtering and muttering even in his sleep. That's when I decided he must be a mocking bird.

He would sit for long periods of time on my shoulder while I was at the computer, cleaning his new feathers and making those silly noises. When he grew bored he'd reach over and peck my ear or my cheek or pull my hair. After his feathers grew in and he began to stretch his wings out and shake them, I took him 3 streets over where there were lots of trees and I knew there were no cats to let him out of the cage. I threw him gently up into the air where he thunked down on the grass like a giant beetle and then walked around pecking and exploring like some chicken. He just wanted to walk and peck at things.

When I could see it was going nowhere I caught him up again and put him in the cage to take back home for the day. Sometimes he played little games like hopping under my car and I had to lie down on my stomach and try to coax him out. Luckily there were no people around to watch us. This went on for a week, with me taking him out morning and evening to try and get him to fly. I was vainly waiting for the empty nest syndrome to set in but he wouldn't cooperate.

Finally one morning I threw him up in the air and he flew a long ways horizontally across the grass and through the trees, landing…you guessed it… on the ground where he starting pecking and poking again. I retrieved him and the next morning I brought him out and again threw him in the air. This time he went directly and vertically up into a nice leafy tree and disappeared. I returned the next morning expecting to see him on the ground gleaning again, but I swear I heard him high up in the tree, squawking and muttering like he always did and sadly but happily too, he must have decided he was a bird.

9.

HEROES

I need heroes—most everyone does. But I have noticed that while I was sitting still, many of my beloved Hollywood stars have grown practically ancient or passed away? How could they do that to me? How and when did they become wrinkled and old? How many times have I wished with all my heart that they didn't feel compelled to make that last movie, act on that last TV program. Time has not treated many of them kindly. So many Hollywood greats have died; that is sad. It is hard to witness the passing of the greats, no matter what age, but in their 80s and 90s we don't want to see them leave us. They serve to remind us of our own mortality.

Even our favorite Hollywood animals are deserting us. Hardly anyone remembers Rin Tin Tin. Roy Roger's Trigger is stuffed in a museum. Lassie has been through several generations, and now is probably gender confused, since they have switched so often from males to females down the years. Mr. Ed, where are you?

Sports heroes often disappoint us. Political hero is an oxymoron. But Hollywood stars have always shone with their own special light, bigger than life, doing mostly as they please, and we have accepted them with all their moles and warts. Ingrid Bergman is a prime example of how our world views have changed regarding heroes. We loved her, put her on a pedestal for the strong, heroic, moral women she played, and we expected her private life to deserve our worship. When it didn't, we ostracized her. Now our heroes change mates with impunity, switch sexual life styles, and jump from bed to bed. While most of us no longer look on them with the former innocent adoration that we lavished on stars of earlier years, we still regard them as semi-heroes.

There were times in the past generation when writers were heroes. F. Scott Fitzgerald, Hemingway, Faulkner, Louisa May Alcott, Dorothy Parker, were names that lit up lives, that fed our need to see excellence rise above mediocrity. There were heroes in the music world too: Benny Goodman, Louis Armstrong, Ella Fitzgerald, and Irving Berlin. We used to look on musicians with fondness.

The problem with hero worship today is that it is so fleeting. With the news media providing us much more details than we really want to know, nothing is private, sacred or secret anymore. The moment we carve out a hero, we learn he or she has feet of clay. Mud, really, by the time the news media gets through with them.

Not long ago a basketball star spoke on television, stating emphatically that he had no intention of being anyone's role model. He was paid to play basketball and that was it. No one should expect him to live up to any standards other than those he chose. Is that possible, I wonder? Are famous people, no matter what made them famous, allowed to make that decision without considering what facade they show the world?

How much do those we made famous owe us, the public? One female singer said when people ask for her autograph while she is in a restaurant eating, she doesn't consider that an infringement on her time. It was her fans who allowed her to buy three luxury mansions and trips to travel to Europe and to be able to spend thousands of dollars on a lavish wedding.

On the other foot, a young, beautiful country western singer, newly rich and famous, said she was so sick of her fans pestering her that she and her husband were going to purchase a home in Switzerland so no one could find her.

How many religious leaders have we looked up to in awe and reverence only to find they played at being moral and seemed to take glee in duping the public out of their hard-earned cash?

It seems to me that becoming rich and famous has tradeoffs. One is lack of privacy. The other is, you are up there for kids to see as an example whether you like it or not. If you choose not to care, it's something you have to live with. It certainly never bothered Mike Tyson or many of the rock stars to set a poor example of living.

One day, as we become more cynical and less naïve, we won't have heroes, I suppose. They are becoming scarcer and scarcer with each passing year.

POLITICALLY CORRECT

I bought a leather jacket, couldn't afford one new.
It was Salvation Army's finest—fit like a good shoe.
The first time I wore the thing, it caused a helluva stir
Around the collar, everyone saw F-U-R, fur.

It was politically incorrect, they told me to my face,
for killing innocent animals, I was in disgrace.
I tried to scream above the shouts, dodged eggs far too slow
Whoever killed the animals did it 20 years ago!

Blame it on the system, where do they find the words?
To dump the guilt on everyone is really quite absurd.
Could it be a cover-up for greedy politicians?
We rattle pots and pans and they burn down the kitchen.

I voted every year I could, most times the pickings lean.
But it never seemed to change a thing--politics are mean.
If you don't vote, for shame, that's politically incorrect.
No matter the measly choices, you must show respect.

Do your patriotic duty, to further their careers.
Show political correctness though you land upon your rear.
So Social Security and Medicare need massive resurrection
Fight their wars and don't protest—that's political incorrection.

Blame it on the system, where do they find the words?
To dump the guilt on everyone is really quite absurd.
Could it be a cover-up for selfish politicians?
While we rattle pots and pans, they're burning down the kitchen.

OPIUM OF THE MASSES

A crowd of thousands stand at attention, their heads bowed, eyes closed against the bright sunlight. A prayer and then a song lift toward heaven with the help of the amplifiers. The voice intones a benediction that threatens to reach its destination by sheer force of volume. When the prayer and song are finished, the crowd continues to stand, watching in rapt attention.

Their attitude is of sheer reverence with interest focused at the side of the amphitheater where the objects of their adoration and devotion will emerge.

As the side door opens, the crowd raises its voice in a tumultuous celebration of praise and glorification. Below the stands, the subjects of the adulation throw up their hands in gestures of benevolent blessing. With a collective sigh, the crowd of ten thousand worshipers sits down and the vast arena grows hushed and silent.

It is opening day of the World Series.

When Karl Marx stated so long ago that religion was the opium of the masses he didn't have baseball, football, basketball, tennis and golf to reckon with. In short, sports are now the opium of the masses.

Do we heap million dollar wage contracts on the heads of our inventors, teachers, or scientists? Would we good-naturedly forgive our astronauts or church leaders for example, if they were caught abusing steroids, doing drugs, or breaking other laws and generally making fools of themselves as some of our sports figures do?

When the players went on strike during baseball season televisions all across America were draped in black. The consumption of nachos and onion dip went down to zero. Budweiser and Coors were gearing up to hire their own teams before the companies became back flushed with left over beer.

In what other area would we make national heroes of spoiled little men who never grew up and use language foul enough to make referees blush? Just because they happen to play good tennis.

Most of us can think of at least one Cro-Magnon who can't remember how many Ten Commandments there are and thinks the Declaration of Independence is something cooked up by woman's lib. But just ask this same person who won the World Series in 1939, or what Babe Ruth's batting average was compared to Joe DiMaggio's, and he can dredge up statistics that would make a computer nerd turn green with envy.

Think about two grown men standing in a little squared off altar above the crowds, pummeling one another like Roman gladiators. The spectators scream with joy at every crunch of bone against flesh, yell with delight at the first sign of blood and jeer their unforgiveness when one of the men fails to rise from being knocked to the floor in semi-consciousness. Instead of appreciating the boxer for the beating he took, the crowd is yelling for that poor sucker to get off his smashed nose and go another round!

Golfers are a breed apart. They have a hidden low self esteem combined with a smugly masochistic pomposity that presumes the entire world is waiting breathlessly for their birdies, bogies and eagles. They love to play in rain and court disaster by holding firmly to their mashie iron while lightning zags downward and thunder shakes the soaking greens beneath their feet. Any fool knows where the term "sudden death" comes into golfing.

Sunday afternoons are famous for long, tedious television specials with men and women solemnly walking over the same route, hitting a little ball into the defenseless trees, big blobs of misplaced deserts and puddles teeming with mosquito larvae. Announcers whisper into microphones, their voices so loud it sounds like drops of spittle on a hot iron. The unexcited crowd is ordered to silence as someone lifts his club and slams into a little ball perched on a piece of wood called a tee. For this, the participants receive thousands of dollars on a weekend.

We hold the Olympics in reverence and anyone not interested in watching every event on television is regarded suspiciously as a possible foreign agent or worse. Never mind that marriages fall apart from neglect, children are ignored, dogs are kicked for barking at the wrong time and the television stays on until everyone has square eyes and fannies to match.

Opium of the masses? Wouldn't Karl Marx have been amazed at the turn we have taken?

WHERE HAVE ALL OUR HEROES GONE?

Where have all our heroes gone?
Randolf Scott, Liberace, Rock Hudson, and
the epitome of perfection, Cary Grant—
seem to be made of different clay.

Is it coincidence—woman's most romantic fantasies,
those we have long adored from afar
are not women-lovers at all—but are gay?
What does that tell us? That we can never
surmount the barriers against us? That we shouldn't care?

How many of us make that same mistake in life?
Falling in love with a need that consumes us—
Only to find it was window dressing
—created from our own fantasy world, like the
elegant body on an emaciated mannequin.

Do we cling stubbornly to our ideals,
like moths throwing fragile bodies against the window--
wanting so badly to be let inside—without knowing why.
Do we instill more deceptions into our psyches, with the
bittersweet taste of ashes on our tongues
each time we swallow another lie?

How is it men and women are supposed to fit together
when there is a discrepancy between what is real and what is ideal
and what we each have to work with?

As mothers, when are we going to teach our daughters
that dreams can never measure up to reality
and more important, teach our sons that
reality must be enhanced by dreams.
And yet we hope, we dream. Some of us give up,
some of us settle, some of us win.
Some are able to show our partners that when we win, so do they.

When that happens we may be able to exist
in a world without heroes.

"Women Should Keep Their Place"

Not long ago I read a letter to the editor of our local paper written by a man I'll call Bill. He wrote a bitter tirade, quoting the Bible in every sentence, about how all the woes of today's world happened because women did not keep their place.

Bill asked the question, why were we involving women like Hillary, Mrs. Dole and Janet Reno, and others of their ilk, to head our bureaus when few women down through history have ruled, but were meant to have the role of support. He went on to quote the Bible, in Genesis, "In sorrow thou shalt bring forth children; and thy desire shall be to thy husband and he shall rule over thee." He claimed history showed that anything other than this policy has proved disastrous to every nation.

He went on to quote Paul in the New Testament, "But I suffer not a woman to teach, nor to usurp authority over the man, but to be in silence." And his quotes go on and on. Then he said that the single family household has caused a disastrous rate of juvenile delinquency without a strong male at the head of the family, and that without a strong male at the head of a nation, the ship hasn't a clear sense of direction.

Is this man living in the present century? It seems to me he would be the first to light a torch under Joan of Arc, or, as king, have a wife beheaded when he could no longer get an heir from her, or maybe change the entire religion of a nation because of his love life.

My answer to Bill was that if he was so big on literal translations of the Bible, didn't he know that Eve was taken from Adam's rib, as God's manifesto that woman was supposed to walk at the side of man. If God had wanted women to walk two steps behind men, it seems as if He, in His infinite wisdom, would have created women from Adam's backside.

Why shouldn't capable women rule? Down through the history, beginning with Biblical times, how many women started wars? How many children have women slain by starvation in Africa and mortar fire in Bosnia? How many females were equal to Hitler, Attila the Hun, and Stalin?

We know of mothers who kill their children. There are women on death row, waiting to die for their crimes. But we are talking *magnitude* here. How many men did women victimize in the way of serial killers starting from Jack the Ripper to Ted Bundy?

From the beginning of time, was it women who decimated thousands of animal and plant species from the earth for profit, greed and carelessness? Give me the name of the woman who invented Teflon bullets or built the nuclear bomb.

You see, Bill, man could do much worse than have woman at his side. The women you, and men like you, have held down through the ages were not allowed to contribute their principles, wisdom or compassion to our civilization.

Now we have more input in our lives and in our world. We do not create single parent families on our own. It is the responsibility of both the man and woman to maintain a home and marriage.

We don't want to walk in front of man, nor behind him; we wish to walk alongside. One day—not yet, but one day—men will understand that by joining with women instead of being threatened by them, men can enjoy an exhilarating, exciting full partnership that will enrich and bless generations to come.

WHY IS IT?

Americans love contentious, crusty old cranks. You know the kind. Remember Andy Rooney of Sixty Minutes, and the movie, "Grumpy Old Men."? They didn't get enough grump out of the first one so they had to make a sequel. Paul Harvey was getting there, only he's still a bit too cheerful.

Since there doesn't seem to be any female-type grumps, I want that job. Maybe I'm not old enough to be a confirmed grump yet, since Mr. Rooney probably was on board to grouse about how Noah was running the Ark. But I'm getting there, and everyone knows women never tell the truth about their age anyway.

I don't want to complain about politics, or far-out religions that pester people at airports or why a car door makes a funny noise when it slams on your fingers. I want to talk about important things.

Like **New and Improved**. Does that phrase make you cringe, set your teeth on edge? It should. Every item that has ever been made "new and improved" is ready for re-cycling.

When did it happen that coffee went from containers of sixteen ounces to twelve ounces? Wasn't anyone paying attention? Now the sugar distributors have been trying for years to flim-flam us with four pounds of sugar and we all know sugar belongs in a five pound wrapper. They finally succeeded. That's their game, to suck the public into getting used to losing that extra pound of sugar. They know we let them get away with it with our coffee.

Have you noticed chicken lately? We were unceremoniously steered away from beef (no pun intended) and our well-marbled steaks went by the way of the buttered croissant. But now that we are buying more chicken, they are loading it with fat. There is fat under the skin, fat along the edges like glistening golden fringes of soft sponge, huge chunks of it under the thighs. The last time I cut up a fryer, I ended up with a double handful of pure fat to throw away. Maybe the growers ought to put the chickens on Atkins diet.

How about cat food? I've bought the same popular brand of dry cat food for a lifetime of cats. It's always been a seven pound sack for an x amount of dollars. Just lately the manufacturer came out with a 6.3 pound sack of the same cat food for the same price. Who do they think we are? Cement brained? After using their 1-800 number to tell some robot answering machine what I thought of the whole idea, I'm switching brands after thirty years. Maybe they won't miss me. Maybe they will.

Why is it they put hot dogs up in twelve packs and hot dog buns in 10s? That took a lot of talent. And why is it we have to pump our own gas, get no windshield wipes or service at all and we pay zillions more for gas?

What about broccoli? Despite an ex-president who hates it, some of us enjoy broccoli. Who among us wants to pay over $1 a pound for 2 inch chunks of white inedible stems we have to buy to get the good stuff? Wonder what they'd say if I brought along my kitchen shears and cut off the portion that I wanted to buy, the portion I am able to eat?

And plastic wrap? TV ads show soup upside down in a cup without spilling, covered with plastic wrap. Don't try it! The only thing plastic wrap clings to is more plastic wrap. Ever try to peel it apart when two edges come together? It's easier to separate two pit bulls with an attitude problem.

I used a popular dishwashing liquid for more years than I'd ever want to admit. Then it came out new and improved. Where it used to sludge out of the plastic bottle like lotion, now it squirts out like water. It used to stay soapy until every last pot and pan was finished and now it lies down and falls asleep before I get the glasses washed. Where it virtually absorbed grease, now it scums along the top of the water, joining in with the grease particles so that through the process of osmosis, they become indestructible.

Dog groomers. Why is it when you bring your precious little bundle in at 7AM you never get him back until way past noon, a span of five or six hours? If they take 10 dogs in from 7am to 8am, for example, do they clip every dog at the same time? Bathe them at the same time? Dry them? It seems to me five hours in a pet groomers are an inordinate amount of time to leave your pet. I'd hate to sit five hours in a beauty salon just to get my hair washed and cut, yet we calmly allow the dog groomers to get away with it. I've often thought to get a job at a pet groomers just to get to the bottom of this puzzle.

Getting back to food, one of my favorite subjects, why is it that flour manufacturers managed to take out every bit of nutrient, every last grain of anything remotely wholesome, and now re-fortify it with most of the vitamins and minerals that they took out in the first place. What was the point? They do the same with milk.

Why is it that hair color products which henna, bleach and dye your hair with fifty different shades and colors are also the largest producers of hair care products like creams that put the life back into dry, dull hair and rinses that are supposed to get inside hair shafts and penetrate the barriers caused by over-bleaching and dying. It seems to me hair companies make money coming and going. Even if your hair all falls out, they have that covered with scalp conditioners.

Cranky old men beware. I've thought of things that are so irksomely irritating, I've barely scratched the surface.

10.

GOING NOWHERE....
TAKING FOREVER TO GET THERE

We did a lot of traveling in our married life. Luckily, by the time we married, Andy had graduated from tenting and backpacking to trailering. I have always enjoyed my creature comforts. Roughing it never held any allure for me. In fact, it is about time to admit that I never even liked traveling. I did it because he wanted to.

First we had an Airstream trailer, and we were called Trailerites. Then we bought a 28' motorhome, which in the 70s was a magic carpet. Now when I see the behemoths on the road, tremendous fifth wheels with slide outs pulled by huge diesel pushers, motor homes the size of a Greyhound bus. It makes me wonder where it is going to end. It was much less complicated in the days of our travels.

We went to Mexico often. In the 60s and 70s it was a charming place, the people delightfully open and friendly. They were glad to see us and we them. Once on our way back to the States, we became stranded in the little mountain mining town of Zacatecas. The automatic transmission broke down on our motor home. Andy had to take the transmission on a bus to the Dodge dealer in Guadalajara, about two hundred miles away through the <u>Barrancas</u>, the Grand Canyon of Mexico. I stayed with the motorhome, parked in front of the Dodge dealer in Zacatecas.

It occurred to me while I waited that I might be there forever; end my days as wife to a local bull fighter, or as that funny little gringa who talks to herself. No one back home knew where we were. I was planning to call my sister as soon as we crossed the border. Busses were known to drop off into space while traveling the narrow mountain roads of the *Barrancas*.

What if Andy never returned? I wasn't preoccupied with worry. It has always been my way to take one day at a time and not to stress about what you can't fix.

On the second day I ventured out and, in my rusty Spanish made my way through the weekly Mercado. In the two weeks I stayed there, I never saw another *gringo*. Apparently Zacatecas was not on the tourist route.

A boy of about twelve and a girl of ten shyly introduced themselves as Ricardo and Angelina. Each took a hand, taking me on a tour through the market place; teaching me new words and making me say them out loud. Sometimes they stifled polite giggles at my attempts. These were not words I'd learned in high school and college conversational Spanish.

Andy had bought a lot of filette, to take home. The fillet is the tenderloin of beef that Mexican butchers trim out in long rolls. Since our motorhome was up on blocks and the butane refrigerator not operating, the meat was thawing fast. The kid's eyes grew round with wonder when I handed them a plastic shopping bag filled with meat. Normally a housewife buys one chicken wing to go into the stew and the husband gets that because he works.

After that, every day their mother sent them to me with wonderful tamales, tacos, and sopa. I gladly stopped eating from our emergency larder of Spam sandwiches on white bread, and dove into the delicious home-cooked food. I never met the kids' mother; they said they would like to invite me to their house, but their mother was ashamed of where and how she lived. Nothing I could say changed that decision. There were five younger brothers and sisters at home, their father had left years ago, taken off for the United States to find work, and never returned.

I could only guess at how the mother supported her family. The two children loved to eat inside my *casita*, my little house. One day Ricky held up his fork and said, "We have one of these." I rummaged through my silverware drawer and gave them everything I could spare. They were ecstatic and couldn't wait to run home to their mother.

We played dominoes every afternoon when they were out of school and finished with their chores. They usually beat me but sometimes I suspected they let me win.

Andy finally returned with the repaired transmission. With tears in my eyes, I hugged and kissed Ricky and Angel and told them I'd always remember them. The next morning at sunrise, long before we were ready to leave, they were at our doorstep, wearing clean clothes, Ricky's cowlick slicked down, Angel's hair braided neatly and with a message from their mother.

She would "give" her son for $100 and Angel for $50 with her blessing, if we would provide them with good homes and take them with us. I never knew this woman, but I know she didn't want to sell her kids. I knew that she figured that was the only way I'd take them, it made it somehow legal, and besides, $150 would take care of her and the other five kids for a long time.

It was the saddest and hardest thing I've ever had to do, to explain to Ricky and Angel that we couldn't take them. For one thing, we had no home. We traveled full time in our vehicle. Andy had retired after a long life of hard work, and I could never ask him to settle down to take care of someone's children, even if we could get across the border with them. Which we couldn't have. It would have involved years of red tape, and money we didn't have to spend on lawyers.

With a heavy heart, I tried to explain as best I could in halting Spanish. It must have been adequate, for I saw the understanding in their eyes and no recrimination or anger. We had gifts for them and their family, the best we could do.

Although we went through Zacatecas many times on our travels, we never saw Ricky or Angel again.

CO-PILOT

Although Andy generously bestowed on me the designation of Copilot. I never was too good with directions. It took him years to teach me to read a map to his satisfaction. I could hold my own with intricacies of Shakespeare, Walt Whitman and diagramming sentences in English 101, but the logic of map reading escaped me for a long time.

Once in Mexico, in the area of Zacatecas, high in the mountains, I read instructions in our guide book that we must be sure to take the first left turnoff to avoid the truck traffic moving through town. He asked if I was sure. I said; "Of course. would the map lie?"

We turned off with our 28 foot motorhome towing a Datsun station wagon. As we continued, the road became unpaved, began to wind and, what was worse, started to climb sharply upward. There was no way to turn back.

Soon we came upon workers building the road ahead of us. Andy wouldn't stop and ask directions, does any man ever? We continued until we made a curve and below us about two thousand feet down lay Zacatecas, we could barely make out the buildings.

The road ended. Ahead I could see the steep roof of a cathedral. Now I knew where we were. We had taken the little mountain trail up to the Lady of Sorrows Cathedral.

What to do? Luckily Andy stayed cool in a crisis, although by now he was a little tightlipped and I knew I was going to catch a lot of "I told you so's" later, if we ever had a later.

We unhooked the car and pushed it away. Then he commanded me, who had never driven the rig, to get behind the wheel. Did I mention that I was afraid of heights?

There I was, sitting high in the driver's seat thousands of miles over nowhere with only the huge windshield between me and oblivion. It was the worst moment of my life. Andy knew I was scared, so he stood in front on a tiny ledge of earth and I could only see his hands. He said he would direct me and if I made a mistake, we would go together.

Somehow that wasn't much comfort.

I put the vehicle in reverse and backed up, slowly, inches at a time, into the side of the mountain until I heard crunching noises, then I slowly moved forward inch by inch, keeping my eyes from the empty chasm in front of me and seeing only his hands in the air, as he stood on the edge of the precipice, motioning me forward or back.

Andy was way ahead of his time and had recently installed a Perkins Diesel engine in what previously was a 357 gas engine with Automatic transmission. That probably saved our lives. I doubt I could have managed to control a gas engine with an automatic transmission.

However the high altitude was making this one sputter and balk at times, which wasn't helping my terror.

After about an hour of agonizing inching backward and forward, we managed to turn the vehicle around and point it on the trail downward. Our tail pipe was crunched as was our back bumper and there was considerable damage to the holding tanks, but that was minor.

Many years later, friends told us of sitting in a café in Zacatecas watching these stupid gringos make their way up to see the Cathedral. I never told them we were the stupid gringos.

COLORADO CAMPING

Of course Andy couldn't say too much. He'd gotten us in a few hairy scrapes, too.

When we had the 24 foot Airstream Trailer, he used to travel highways and byways, never on the freeways, if he could help it. He always looked for the new adventure, the great experience. He had to know what was on the other side of the mountain.

I didn't have to know that, I had already figured out it was just another mountain, but then I never claimed to be adventurous. Sometimes I think it would be a good idea if couples worked these notions out before the "I do's".

While we were eating breakfast at a little cafe in Colorado, a sweet-faced elderly couple in the next booth told us about a fantastic, bottomless volcanic lake that was in a beautiful secluded campground.

Andy checked the map and it looked okay. A few curves in the road, a couple of switchbacks, a little altitude, but nothing major.

Before the advent of these light footed SUVs, many of us 'trailerites' as we called ourselves, used International Travel-Alls to pull our rigs. It took our vehicle the better part of the day to climb that mountain. On switchbacks, and sharp curves where the trailer rear was out over air, miles below the river looked like a silver necklace. I looked only once and that was enough. On the single lane road it was my job to reach over and blow the horn frequently, in case someone was coming down. There were small pullouts here and there, but at that point, I didn't think Andy was going to be maneuvered into using one. He was intent on staying in the middle.

When we finally topped the mountain, people rushed out to greet us. We climbed out on shaky legs and saw only cars and tents. The campers marveled that we were the first ever to haul a trailer up that road.

It was a lovely place. The lake was fathomless and black, and the silence in the pine-surrounded woods was heavenly. It took Andy two weeks to work up courage for the trip down. To tell the shameful truth, if it hadn't been such a long way, I would have walked it. We got up at the crack of dawn to be sure we wouldn't meet anyone coming up. He put the vehicle in low gear and I honked and prayed all the way to the bottom.

Even after all these years I would enjoy getting my hands on that sweet-faced couple. They had to have been serial killers in disguise.

One good thing came of it. Andy never again razzed me about my inadequate map reading abilities.

TRIPLE A CAMPGROUND

We had a penchant for getting into places that we could barely get out of.

On a hot summer weekend we turned off from the freeway heading east and went looking for a campground designated A-1 by our guide book.

It was just out of Houston, Texas. We read it was supposed to be nestled near a lake with huge trees and picnic spots, an idyllic place, if there ever was one. We had the motorhome and were towing the little Datsun station wagon.

When we pulled onto the road to the campground it began to narrow. It had recently rained and there were huge potholes hidden beneath puddles; and muddy places near the edge of the road that looked as if we could get stuck forever in the mire. By the time we found the campground it was near dusk. A family ran over and asked us if we were planning to stay. They had just come for the day and were leaving.

We told them about our guide book whereupon they informed us that this was a notorious hangout for city gangs during weekends. All the regular travelers went to the campground on the other side of the lake where there were police patrols all night.

By then it had started to rain and it was getting dark fast. We followed the family out and they disappeared when we took a wrong turn and ended up in a cul-de-sac.

There was nothing to do but stop and unhook the car so we could turn the motor home around. I was going to drive the car until we got out on the highway and found the other road to the legitimate campground.

Wouldn't you know the battery was dead in the Datsun? I couldn't start it. When we tried to push it out of the way so we could turn the big rig around, I dropped the keys in a huge mud puddle.

Just then a carload of Hispanic youths pulled up and sat watching in creepy silence. We didn't know what to do. Andy always carried a gun when we traveled, but it was in the motor home, tucked away under the bed. The leader got out and sauntered over to assess the situation. The rain had stopped, but it was getting darker by the moment. The thought came to me that we could die here and our families would never know what happened to us.

The young man popped his gum and stared at us for a long moment. Through his eyes, I saw our expensive looking rig, the extra car and our complete vulnerability. Finally, as if coming to a decision, he motioned for the guys to get out of their car and come over. Andy and I stood close together. I could tell by the way his jaw clenched that he figured we were in for a bad time.

Without a word, the boys went up to the Datsun and pushed it out of the mud, away from the motor home so Andy could make the turn. Meanwhile I knelt at the edge of the mud puddle to fish for the keys.

All this time no one spoke. I croaked out that I'd lost my keys so the boys wouldn't think I'd gone bonkers. I felt the keys at the edge of my fingers and held them up triumphantly.

Big white smiles creased their faces and they got behind the Datsun again to push me off so it would start.

When the engine caught, I had a tiny urge to keep going down that road lickety-split, but of course I didn't. I backed up, left it idling, and as the youths turned to get back in their car, Andy and I followed them to shake their hands. We thanked them and Andy offered them money, but they shook their heads and took off toward the forbidden campground, wheels spinning.

We didn't stop at the other campground, but decided to move on toward Louisiana.

THE ARMADILLO from AMARILLO

If you live in Amarillo, it's very plain to see,

You must have an Armadillo, to keep you company.

No ordinary dog or cat... no hamster or gorilla...

Oh, if you live in TEXAS, it's strictly Armadilla.

They're good at hunting golf balls, in holes made of sand,

They use them at the borders, to sniff out contraband.

They like them for retrievers, when they hunt for ducks.

And all the spotted ones are used, just on fire trucks.

They're great at catching mice; they eat up all the bugs.

In gardens, they adore aphids, snails and slugs.

Mexicans love bullfights, Texans have their own of course,

When fighting Armadillos, it takes a very little horse.

There are a million reasons why Texans love these critters.

They're brave and very loyal, make terrific baby sitters.

So raise your glass and sing a toast from Waco to Amarillo

And pray that Texas always has their precious Armadillo.

MEXICAN HAT DANCE

We traveled all over Mexico in the late 60s, but finally settled on a favorite area. Guadalajara. It was a lovely city, gracious and old-fashioned. Streets were narrow and lined with gigantic Jacaranda trees spilling blossoms of pink and pale lilac through their sparse leaves.

Each year we returned to a little trailer park (in those days we didn't aspire to call them RV parks) on the outskirts of town where we met acquaintances and friends that we'd been seeing for years.

The gardener was named Pancho. He was taciturn and serious for the most part, always dressed in the same clean brown shirt and pants. No one ever saw him without his sombrero. You could tell he was very proud of that hat.

One lazy afternoon I decided, with my typical warped sense of humor, to have a little fun with Pancho. Andy had a beat-up old straw hat he'd bought seasons before in the market place and he'd been threatening to throw it away for a long time. We went out on the patio where Pancho was kneeling, digging in the flowers.

"I'm so sick of this hat! You never throw anything away. It's useless!" I yelled at Andy. Then I proceeded to throw it down on the cement patio and do my version of a Mexican hat dance around it. When I was sure I had Pancho's full attention, I jumped with both feet, right in the middle of that straw hat, squashing it beyond redemption.

For a brief second all we heard was Pancho's indrawn breath and the echo of the crackled straw beneath my feet.

He looked at Andy, probably expecting him to backhand me or at the very least berate me. When Andy didn't do anything, except try to stifle his laughter, Pancho got to his feet, shook his head and walked away muttering to himself.

Ever afterward he never worked in our yard when our car was there and I swear I heard him muttering under his breath every time he passed us, "*Loco gringos.*"

ALASKA

My favorite place to live has got to be Alaska. It is not a state, nor a region nor anything else you can put a handle on; it is a state of mind. You either love it or hate it, there is no in between.

We took a trip up the Alcan Highway to Anchorage to visit my sister and her husband. He was stationed at Elmendorf Air Base in Anchorage. They eventually transferred them to the Lower 48, but we stayed another four years.

We drove up in time to get in on all the aftershocks of that great earthquake of 1963. On our way up we crossed bridges with our loaded Airstream trailer towed by an International Travel-All and held our breath at the signs that warned, "Don't slow down or stop on bridge, don't shift gears, and don't put on brakes." Meaning the bridges were about to collapse from earthquake damage and the highway department hadn't had time to repair them.

Back in Canada yet, we broke two axels on the International before Andy thought to examine our load in the back. I'd been a rock hound for many years and while in Mexico I found a stash of beautiful sheen obsidian, really fine specimens. I didn't bother to tell Andy when I stashed them in the back. They probably weighed quite a bit and when he discovered the box, he gave me a dirty look and threw them out on the side of the road. Probably for a long time travelers finding them marveled as to how volcanic residue such as obsidian turned up along the Alcan Highway.

In Anchorage it was dark in the winter when we went to work in the morning and dark when we got out of work at 5:00. Many times we walked down 4th Avenue, the main street, eating an apple on our lunch hour and tossing it away when it became frozen half way through the eating.

From the huge picture window in the bank lobby the customers could see an alleyway with shacks just behind Main Street. There was a rickety old stairway going up to a second story loft where men made a steady stream up and down. It was a "lady of the night" plying her trade during lunch hour.

Drinking and going to parties were favorite pastimes in Alaska. I worked in a bank and from a bar down the street came flyers almost every day advertising after work specials. They celebrated ground hog day, Bastille day—any day was a special day to celebrate up there. And high rollers—it is hard to know whether the gamblers came up there because of who and what they were, or if Alaska made them that way.

I had a real estate broker friend who took her vacation "out" or "stateside" as they called the lower 48s. She saved all year to go to Las Vegas and stayed until she lost her bundle, which was considerable. She played day and night, seldom slept or ate and came back exhausted, broke and perfectly content. Ready to do it all again her next vacation.

We learned to cross-country ski which, in the early days before the ski-mobile, was a serene, beautiful sport. Going out into the snow covered countryside with the silence surrounding like a blanket of white was an experience I am thankful for. We took our lunch and a bottle of wine in our backpacks. When we were tired and hungry, we stopped, leaned against a snow drift to eat and drink.

The snow is normally very dry and won't melt even when you sit on it. Once a whiteout came upon us and we were terrified, but it passed after an hour so we could see to get home. The whiteout is an eerie mist—the terror of pilots and anyone else out on the tundra. Everything turns white with an ice fog and you can't see your hand in front of your face.

We had a neighbor who lived across the street from us. Everyone called him Crazy Vukovitch—certifiable, for sure. He was the only man who would take a bulldozer out at low tide and scrape out the sound below Anchorage for boat moorings. Once he went too far out and the crowd that always gathered to watch him saw his bulldozer slowly sink down and down into the ooze. He stayed on like he was riding a bronco at a rodeo until the last minute and then climbed off and waded through the mud to shore.

He was a bush pilot and a guide, one of the last of those wild breeds. His partner went out hunting one time and unfortunately walked on a grizzly's pathway. Vukovitch found his body scattered here and there when he went looking for him. He waited on the bear path and sure enough the bear challenged him—the biggest grizzly he had ever seen. The bear skin stretched all the way across his double-wide mobile home, and part way up the walls on both sides.

In summer the daylight lasted except for a few hours in the middle of the night when it was semi-dark. Elmendorf Air Force Base was just on the outskirts of Anchorage, and you could see the airmen, all hours of the night, walking around Anchorage, probably because the light confused them and they thought they should still be awake.

In Matanuska Valley, a few miles from Anchorage, farmers grew fifty pound turnips because of the rich soil and constant light in the summer. I thought at the time that a fifty pound turnip should be outlawed. Yuck!

We were there before overpasses and freeways and skyscrapers. You couldn't walk around downtown without meeting a dozen people you knew, and half of them stopped to invite you to a party. Most of us made our own brew and we had the best tasting beer around. It was so strong that many times we wound up with many of the bottles broken with the pressure. When a party was in the offing, we tossed bottles out in the snow to cool down. In spring thaw we found broken bottles under the melting snow of those we hadn't removed in the winter.

I have never returned to Anchorage because I want to remember it the way it was—the most beautiful place in the world.

I wrote several poems about Alaska, but only one song.

LITTLE LOG SHACK
(to the tune of Little Grass Shack in Hawaii)

Take me back to my little log shack in Chugiak, Alaska,

Where the sun never shines and the wind blows all day long.

It's the only place I know of where the caribou and moose

grow almost as big as mosquitoes, and they let the bears run loose.

Oh, I dream every night of the moonlight on the ski slopes.

I love the jade and ivory and moose nuggets best of all.

I'm just a homesick little Alaskan girl, to see that Big Dipper flag unfurl.

I wanna go back to my little log shack in old Chugiak.

Fool's Gold in Alaska

Do you mind if I ask ya, did you come from Alaska?
I can tell by your look blue and cold.
From Fairbanks to Nome, many a fool's left home,
searching for that thing called gold.

When the cold damp wind crawls under your skin,
and the wolves are on the prowl.
You can thank the Lord you're not outside in
the midst of the blizzard's howl.

Oh, a hard rock claim or a placer stake
or flour gold from the creek
—It's all the same, this thirst for gold,
no room for the mild and weak.

But the pure, crisp air that riffles your hair
and the silence of woods and snow
With the moon, pale and strange over the mountain range
—will never let you go.

When the ice fog clings to all wooded things
in a pattern of dainty lace.
White mountains arise to join bright blue skies....
There just is no other place.

11.

VOLUNTEERING- CASA
(COURT APPOINTED SPECIAL ADVOCATE)

WINDOWS OF OPPORTUNITY

I first heard that phrase used by a doctor, many years ago. Now it has become a cliché with use. When an operation goes bad, for example, there is a limited time in which a surgeon can correct the mistake, make things right again, before nerves, tissues and sinew deteriorate.

Do we have Windows of Opportunities in our lives? I think it must be so. Sometimes we can return to correct a mistake, ease harsh words, and apologize for errors made. We should take advantage of our Windows of Opportunities before it is too late, before the rifts are unapproachable.

Most times we don't. One window of opportunity comes if we choose to do something for the community, to give back a portion of the emotional riches, the knowledge we've gained through the years. Whatever our childhood experience, at this stage we've survived, and what a good thing it is to share our enthusiasm with those who need a lift. It becomes a true window of opportunity that stays longer and longer and finally refuses to close.

WHAT IS A CASA?
(Court Appointed Special Advocate)

The boy sits alone in a room, he is waiting. . .
his clothes are still stuffed in a black plastic bag.
This house is so quiet, he misses the turmoil
that was part of his life for all of his past.
He waits in a room that is not his room...
He sits in a house where he'll never belong,
he waits for the pieces to come back together,
he knows this must happen, he wants to go home.
He thinks if he's still, he thinks if he's good,
they'll see in his heart --words he can't say.
The boy has no CASA.

Bruised from a beating, the frail little girl
enters a court room afraid and alone.
What can she tell them? How can she lie?
But she dare not tell the truth, she can't snitch
on her parents, they are her family....
And what of her sisters? Who will get them
ready for school if these people take her?
She needs a friend she can talk to,
She needs a CASA.

The screaming, the fighting, the tight, scared feeling
comes every weekend when Daddy gets home.
In spite of his drinking, they want to go back,
it's their only security,
their home is their anchor in a world
that is spinning--out of control.
Four children displaced, separated by strangers
for their good, it is said,
but how could they know?
They could talk to a CASA.

Six fosters he's lived with, in his nine years.
They say he is troubled, they say he is mean.
He wants to go home, he can ignore the beatings,
he can hide from the fighting, it's where he belongs.
He misses his sisters, he misses his brothers,
he survives in a world that he's helpless to change.
He wants to spit out his anger to someone
who'd listen--without hating him back—
Where is the CASA?

She cares for her family, her brothers and sisters,
she cleans up her mother when she's sick on drugs,
Eight going on thirty, she'll never be young again,
Her childhood is gone along with her dreams.
But one day a stranger came by to listen,
And keeping her promise, she stopped by again.
The girl found an adult she could tell of her troubles,
To spill out her fears, she'd discovered a friend.
She found a CASA.

We listen, we pray, we try to fit in with the lives
of the children who have lost all their trust
in adults and their promises, in a system that is too slow.
So much time passes that can never be replaced
in a child's life that is measured in minutes, not years.
If, as CASAs we offer a respite of peace,
a shoulder to cry on, a period of listening,
if we can form a bridge between the worlds of
insanity, instability, terror and pain
by just being there--that is a CASA.

*IF SOMETIMES WE FEEL LIKE A BAND-AID ON AN OPEN
ARTERY...
REMEMBER WHAT HAPPENS...WITHOUT THE BAND-AID.*

Your Little Bird Spirit"

Each of us has within
a little bird spirit
to fly free.
Some of us have a hole
in the heart of
our little bird spirit
so we cannot soar and
flap our wings.
The hole in our heart is an
opening to call in bad
thoughts, anger and fear.
Sometimes our beaks get
hurt and it's hard
to make a sound out loud
so we grow
silent and still—
forgetting how to sing.

We must learn to heal our
little bird spirits—
to heal our beaks and hearts
by sitting in the moonlight
and soaking up the healing power
of the soft warm light—
by trusting enough to
let a Higher Power come
close and touch
our little bird spirit
to bring us comfort
and peace.
When we close the hole in
our heart and make it well,
fill the emptiness
with joy and harmony,
—we learn to fly again.

—For children everywhere

COURT APPOINTED SPECIAL ADVOCATE -- (CASA)

I've never been a joiner, but the time came in my life when I wanted to repay a debt to my community for blessings received over the years. After watching over older people in my neighborhood for many years, I wanted a change. I wanted to help children, to help reunite them with their family or to help find a better place for them.

If my plan was to sacrifice time, effort and caring, my plan backfired. My CASA family has given me much more than I could ever repay. The kids are sweet, vulnerable, loving and I am sort of a surrogate grandmother to them. Since I've never been a grandmother, it turned out to be an exciting, enlightening, shiny-new experience.

I had reached a point where kids annoyed me. I couldn't relate to them, mentally heaping them all together in a scrap pile of selfish, domineering, rude little people, without seeing them as individuals. Since I have learned to open up to my CASA kids, I still see some children as selfish, domineering and rude, but as individuals, not as a race of little people who are all the same.

My CASA kids are so complex--filled with joy and spirit, in spite of being uprooted from their families, put in foster homes, one after another, set adrift in a world without walls, a world that held no certainties. For the most part, the fosters were great, loving families who gave to the little strangers in their midst, but it wasn't their family. And yet these kids didn't turn mean or bitter or hateful. They kept it inside, trusting sooner or later that eventually the adults who had control of their lives would somehow come to their senses and make it all right again and they could go home.

And that is the most satisfying, gut-wrenching feeling of all, when it comes together for the family, when the family unit is as mended and workable as it can be, and you know you've had a part in making it happen.

Since my plan of community sacrifice has backfired, I guess I'll just have to choose another file, another family, another set of kids to grandmother and start all over again. How lucky can one person get?

QUOTES ABOUT CHILDREN.

"I love these little people; and it not a slight thing, when they, who are so fresh from God, love us."
>   --Dickens

"A torn jacket is soon mended, but hard words bruise the heart of a child."
>   -- Longfellow

"The first duty to children is to make them happy. If you have not done so, you have wronged them. No other good they may get can make up for that. "
>   -- Buxton

"You save an old man and you save a unit; but save a boy and you save a multiplication table."
>   --"Gipsy" Smith

"Childhood sometimes does pay a second visit to a man; youth never."

>   --Anna Jameson

WHEN LOVE IS NOT ENOUGH

Love is a powerful force in our lives. The lack of it can wreak havoc, emotional and physical, especially in children. In countries where babies were raised in bassinets without parents or anyone to hold them, the babies withered and died or were permanently damaged so that later, when someone wanted to care for them, the children were unable to accept love.

Psychologists have discovered that child neglect is equally as damaging to a delicate, vulnerable spirit as child abuse. In child abuse, the child is getting attention, however misplaced or disturbing, but a child ignored and neglected is harmed with a deep, inner emptiness that can last forever.

The other side of the coin is love given to children without the support of discipline, protection, and nurturing care for their needs.

In our CASA cases, we have seen both sides. Many times we get sucked in to the needs of the parents. They want their children, but cannot care for them adequately and appropriately because of mental illness, drugs and alcohol abuse, finances, lack of ability to cope with day to day problems— there are many reasons a parent will love the child but not be a fit parent.

We are told that we must accept "minimal parenting" and not expect perfection from our cases. Watch out for this trap. Our battle cry is not minimal parenting but is and always will be: "FOR THE BEST INTEREST OF THE CHILD. We cannot, must not, lose that objective though we may pity the parent's dilemma.

A good CASA will agonize over the decision of the S word—Sever. A good CASA will usually have a hard time even saying the word, unless the circumstances are so terrible that severing is an obvious necessity. Sometimes just the mention of "Sever" and "Adopt" in a court report is enough to shock the parent into becoming a capable parent or accepting the facilities available to learn how to become one.

Love is many things to many people. But love from a parent to a child is caring, nurturing, supporting, day by day care that, in the long run, will produce a competent, functional member of society. All parenting should be focused on nurturing a child who will not repeat the circle of welfare, inadequate parenting and the perpetuation of a dysfunctional family.

As a CASA, our decisions must be to insure the child has, at the very least, a chance in life. Sometimes love has to step aside.

12.

AGING GRACEFULLY

Ahead of my time--or behind it?

I should have been a child of the 60s instead of the 50s. It seems I've always been just a little ahead of my time or at least out of step with the times. In school I always had to question, to challenge authority—to ask why, when all I was there for, presumably, was to soak up knowledge like a sponge—passively and offer no resistance.

At that time I was painfully shy, so my stubborn contentiousness was no more than passive rebellion. But now that I am older and no longer shy, but ask my questions with what must be a disconcerting bluntness, I still get only a cold blank stare and no answers.

My husband suggested that on my tombstone should read "Yes...but..." This makes me wonder. Do we all skim along life, staying close to the surface, barely creating a ripple, afraid to make waves, wallowing in our comfort zones?

RED BALLOON

I woke up this morning and saw a red balloon

floating down the street

in search of a child.

Captured within a sterile existence of stone and metal

—Adults Only—retirement village.

Snared in an atmosphere of wrinkles and Geritol,

skipping against memories of grandchildren

a thousand miles away.

The balloon drifted...hopeless and lost

searching—sifting down the street

bouncing with false gaiety like new store teeth

that turns a smile into a wince.

A balloon in search of delighted laughter

and finding only silence.

I woke up this morning and saw a red balloon

floating down the street

in search of a child.

YARD SALE

I stopped at a yard sale a few days ago. A little old lady looking at least one hundred, if a day, sat watching the proceedings. She appeared testy, frustrated, talking to herself as the customers passed by her.

Every time someone picked up an item, the old lady had something to mumble about it. Listening close and pretending not to, I heard her tell where the item came from, how old it was, a kind of general run-on description without ever mentioning herself: as if she struggled to maintain her distance from what was happening: as if she were relating a story about another family, not her own.

The more the shoppers uneasily tried to ignore her, the more she spoke, louder and louder. Some of her speech was intelligible, some garbled, as if the words were too large to say without choking. Often she lost her train of thought, became confused and rambled, but her eyes, sharp and bird-like, stayed fixed on all her belongings spread out on the lawn for God and strangers to see.

A heavyset younger woman, her daughter most likely, was selling the stuff. Harried, yet resolute, she seemed to be reaching a point where she would have given everything away just to be done with it.

Someone held up a box of old frames, with pictures still in them. "Two bucks for the whole box," and the old lady's face crumpled, her thin mouth worked. Nothing came out as if she fought back tears. So angry and resentful was she that she'd never let the strangers or her daughter see her cry. Two dollars for the box full—as if strangers who would toss the pictures and use the frames could purchase memories for two bucks.

A big-handed man rifled carelessly through a box of delicately crocheted doilies, created lovingly with great patience as to the color arrangements and patterns. The old woman's eyes must have strained as, painstakingly with tiny crochet hooks, she completed each piece to adorn couch backs, arms and tables of her home. No flat space ever went bare in her house; that would have been a sign of a neglectful, careless housewife. Hours spent at night squinting to make the tiny stitches while the kids and husband sat listening to the radio. No idle hands—ever.

"Five dollars for the box," the young woman sang out and the old lady muttered, but her words were unintelligible.

Here is this elderly woman, probably headed for a rest home or maybe, reluctantly, with heavy obligation, being provided a little place to live in her daughter's house.

She sits and watches her prized possessions pawed over, examined, discussed at length and bargained down to nothing—while her daughter perseveres doggedly with a job she felt she had to do.

I've pondered on that scene a lot and often wondered—why didn't the daughter get rid of her mother's possessions after she moved away? Why couldn't the daughter have pretended to box up the stuff to keep in storage for her? How much trouble could it have been to store her mother's things away temporarily? Why couldn't she permit the mother a last shred of dignity, of pride?

Was there a hidden agenda, something that the mother did to the daughter sometime during their lifetime together which made the daughter forever passive-aggressive, resentful, unforgiving, waiting her chance to even the score? That idea is somehow preferable to thinking the daughter obtuse and indifferent to the distress of her mother, unknowing that probably at that moment—her mother had already died.

Is there such a disease as terminal averageness bordering on mediocrity? Am I the only one who worries about it? I have all the symptoms of the disease: I play guitar and organ, but not well. I sing, but not exceptionally. I dabble in photography, paint and cook and write prose and poetry—but is there a patina of expertness about any of it?

Do we expect too much of ourselves? Or not enough? Is there any value to examining our lives so constantly when others never seem to bother holding theirs up to scrutiny, but skim over life perfectly content and happy?

We are who we are, I suppose. Some of us were born to wonder what we are here for. Others never do. They are no doubt the lucky ones.

***

Count your blessings like beads on a rosary. All non-blessings are merely the links that hold the beads together. They are not as important in the final scheme of your life as are the beads of your blessings.

***

LOOKING BACK....

I am not a backward looking person. You won't hear me reciting litanies of the "good old days" or even what happened several years ago. What's done is done. I live absolutely in the present.

But sometimes a bit of nostalgia creeps in and I reflect on my high school years. I always saw them as sad, shy, melancholy lonely years. I was never in step, never quite in sync with my peers. For a time I was on a Russian novel kick, devouring every Dostoyevsky and Tolstoy I could get my hands on, reveling in their sense of doom and gloom.

I wrote unhappy, sensitive poetry and liked to be alone with my thoughts and my writing.

This was my perception of my years from fourteen to seventeen. When I came across my senior album from high school recently, I sat down to look at it for the first time in thirty years. Remember how kids write such "meaningful" (or so we thought at the time) words of wisdom or bits of information in each other's annuals?

Imagine my shock when I began to read about how much FUN we had, how much FUN I was to be with—How much these schoolmates enjoyed "my humor and happy temperament" and how I used to instigate amiable rebellion in classes by tormenting my teachers, to the delight of my classmates.

Well...suddenly I felt betrayed, shorn of familiar memories. All this time my years had been sweetly golden and I had chosen to remember them as a vinegary, shadowy blue.

Memories are not trustworthy. We are too selective. Our recollections are veiled and shrouded by a patina of experience, wishful thinking, imagination, perversity, or who knows what manner of aberration and from where it stems.

I think it might be a reasonable conclusion that one should never trust or rely on the memory of anyone over forty.

COMING UP ROSES

Let me tell you how it went today,

    The sand in my hour glass has surely shifted.

I went to town to do some shopping...

    For that, I expect, I am truly gifted.

Lo and behold when I passed by a mirror

    I saw that my tee shirt was inside out.

It wouldn't have mattered quite so much

    But size 2X on the label seemed to shout.

To make matters worse, I have two pairs of tennis.

    One is beige and the other is peach

At the grocery store I happened to notice

    I was wearing one of each!

So I guess what I'm thinking is—it can't be important

    If people are tattooed and wearing rings in their noses

If I remember to put on panties and bra when out shopping

    I'm pretty well coming up roses.

"*No One Needs My Flowers Anymore*"

A garden filled with treasures,

Lovely flowers to be shared—

I left on porches in the early morn

To show that someone cared.

In a neighborhood resides forgotten

ladies past their prime

Some are widows, some have husbands

who've lost track of time.

A Mother's Day remembrance,

Birthdays, special days pass by.

When they find bouquets of flowers

Some smile, and some may cry.

Eventually the ladies fade away,

Passed on to a better place

where they are not forgotten,

where a smile lights up their face.

Now my garden stands neglected,

Roses bloom and die.

The pleasure is there, but something's gone

I can feel the blossoms sigh.

No one needs my flowers anymore.

LIFE'S LITTLE EXASPERATIONS

There are some things in life I just don't understand; like leaf and snow blowers, for example. Where do the owners expect the leaves and snow to go? Do they think because a blast of air takes the debris into space it won't come down again? Is it a perception that once litter is airborne it is no longer anyone's responsibility?

Workers in a business parking lot seem to enjoy using a blower to clean out flotsam and jetsam created from emptied car ashtrays or carelessly thrown wrappers. Way up in the air they go, whee! Landing in the street, in the gutters or on adjoining parking lots. Why can't they use outdoor vacuums? I've answered my own question. Then they would have to look for a place to dump their own residue.

Call waiting is another of life's exasperations. We are so busy and so anxious to talk to everyone that we cannot bear to miss any calls. When you call a friend or family and they say, "Hold on a minute, got another call," or worse, "Gotta hang up, another call is coming in." Does anyone realize how that makes the original caller feel? It's kind of like being picked over like a bag of rags by someone searching for a silk vest in the pile. Especially when you've taken the trouble to call long distance. It must be that a bird in the bush is preferable to a bird in the hand. I'd like to tell them what people get when they have a bird in the hand, but so far I've been too polite.

Speaking of phones, the cell phone is the pits and not just because I don't happen to like mine. At a restaurant the other night a birthday party was underway, the chairs filled with laughing children, wives in their finery, everyone having a great time. Then the Big Kahuna's phone rang and guests had to subside in silence, all eyes focused on him so they could tell when the call was over and they could go back to what they were there for, the party.

It is probably illegal in most states to use the phone in a moving vehicle except for emergency. We all have seen drivers dawdle at green lights or turn a corner on two wheels with the phone clutched in their hand. Ever watch a driver holding a lit cigarette and a cell phone while negotiating traffic in the rush hour? It's scary. Tell you what I think about cell phones, I got fired from a job once because I never turned the thing on.

Did I mention I don't like dried noodles that stick in the glue at the bottom of packages? Does anyone care for the people who go to the fast check out line in a grocery store with a basket full, a check they didn't write out while they waited and with the dim-witted urge to balance their checkbook before they leave the line. These same people never have their I.D. ready. When the clerk looks at them expectantly, light dawns and they begin to search for their driver's license.

Justice would be served if stores had a scanner at the fast check out. When a customer goes over the authorized amount, spot lights beam down with sirens shrieking so that the perpetrator slinks off in disgrace to another line.

Speaking of stores, people who leave their baskets in the middle of the aisle to talk to a neighbor are not my favorite souls. When you touch their basket to move it they glare as if you've violated them personally. Also mothers who tell their children, "Go play with the toys, I'll come back for you," are a joy to behold. The little darlings rip through the blister packs, taking out dolls and toy cars to scatter on the floor until mommy comes to claim them. She never looks back at the toy-carnage left behind. We, as consumers, pay for that little baby sitting trick, and so in the long run does she, but I don't expect her to care.

What happened to us that we have become so self-centered, so me-dedicated? The lamentable thing is, the newest generation has been imbued with their parent's narcissism and arrogance, their disdain for other people's feelings and dignity.

A belief sustains me that there is an inherent cycle of human behavior whereby principles and ethics will come to a full circle and return to our planet. I hope I'm here to see it happen.

Meanwhile, how do I get the noodles out of the pack without breaking them to bits?

Letter to an old friend:

Do you enjoy antiquities too? Going to museums of natural history is pure magic. I've seen the museums in New York and Chicago. And I love graveyards, especially old ones.

Have you done anything on your genealogy?

I found out two of my great grandfathers were in the Civil War (from Wisconsin it would be the wearing of the blue, of course) and sent for the records. The government sent a packet out free, except for mailing charges. It makes fascinating reading.

One of the ancestors, a farmer from Wisconsin, got a hernia from loading rifles after being in service only a few months. He finally, after six years of paper filling and affidavits, signed by everyone including his neighborhood butcher, got the magnanimous sum of $10 a month medical discharge. He lived only about a year after that, so it was canceled. Guess he messed up his chance for a medal or Purple Heart. Don't think they hand them out for hernias.

Don't laugh, I know that is a story about relatively young antiquities, but it's my relative, all the same.

When I was a child, my grandmother used to sing me a song about the Civil War. I think it's lost in the archives by now, and you wouldn't want me singing it to you, although I remember the tune. It's probably over 100 years old by now. Syrupy by our present standards but I can still hear my grandmother's wispy voice singing.

***

Two little boys, had two little toys,
each had a wooden horse. Gaily they played one summer day,
 warriors both, of course.
One little chap, had a mishap, broke off his horse's head
Wept for his toy, then cried with joy when his brave comrade said...

"Do you think I could leave you crying
   while there's room on my horse for two.
Climb up here, Jim, and don't be sighing,
For he'll go just as fast for two.
When we grow up, we'll both be soldiers,
   our horses will not be toys...
      and it may be that we'll remember,
         when we were two little boys."

Long years had passed, The War broke at last.
Proudly they marched away. The battle roared loud,
'midst them in crowd, wounded and dying Jack lay.
Loud rings the cry, a horse dashes by,
Out of the Ranks of Blue. Gallops away, to where Jack lay,
 a voice comes loud and true.

"Do you think I could leave you dying,
   when there's room on my horse for two?
   Climb up here, Jack, we'll soon be flying
 Towards the Ranks of the Boys in Blue."
 "Did you say, Jim, I'm all a-tremble,
 Well, it may be the battle noise...
      or it may be that I remember,
         When we were two little boys."

There are funny sides to being a housewife and aging gracefully.

A Housewife's Lament

Some say the world will end in fire
and some say ice. . . that's nice.
According to the quantum theory of
finite concentration
and inevitable penetration—
I think the world could end—no must. . .
in dust.

The Joys of Aging Gracefully

When I sneeze, I must cross my thighs
and close my mouth so my teeth don't fly.

****

A quote from Henry Ward Beecher rings so true. He said, "A man without mirth is like a wagon without springs. He is jolted disagreeably by every pebble in the road."

We all know people like that; it doesn't have to be Seniors. Young people are famous for lacking a sense of humor. But when we are older, when we have such a short time left on this earth, how much better to go to meet your Maker with a smile not a frown.

Just Do It

Work like you don't need the money

Love like you've never been hurt.

Dance when nobody's watching,

Make mud pies and don't mind the dirt.

Look through eyes of a five-year-old child

Try dessert first and vegetables last.

Dream daydreams that may never come true

Pretend that the past is all passed.

Pick a rose and forget about thorns,

Live today like tomorrow won't come,

Don't forget to tell friends that you love them

Walk in raindrops as well as the sun.

WHEN THE KIDS HAVE LEFT HOME
—WHEN THE LAST DOG DIES

When the kids all have left home and the last dog dies...when our social security and Medicare kicks in, then we can travel—or plant a rose garden—or write that novel.

Patiently we plod through life, most of us scrimping and saving to send our kids through college, even though they might not want to go when the time comes.

We settle for jobs we despise. We may work with people with whom we have nothing in common, spending years of eight hour days, five days a week in limbo...waiting for the two-day weekend. Waiting twenty years for a pension and freedom.

Those are the ants in life. Busy, productive, their minds on automatic, doing what are expected of them. The person who said we lead lives of quiet desperation knew whereof he spoke.

Then there are the butterflies of humankind. Flighty, desperate to be somewhere else, always seeing the grass as greener on the other side, butterflies do not abide by community rules, agendas or conservative conduct.

Butterflies know that life is short and then you die. So they make the best use of time by living for today and letting tomorrow take care of itself. Who is right, the ant or the butterfly? Who is more productive in society? Is it useful or necessary to compare the two lifestyles? Both have compensations and both have serious drawbacks. Do we have a choice who we will be in life, a butterfly or an ant? Are we programmed from the womb to be one or the other?

I guess the plain truth of it is, we need both the ants and butterflies.

I'LL TELL YOU WHEN I'M OLD

Don't talk to me about "this old lady",
Don't say, "You're getting too old for that!"
Never suggest I act my age...
Don't bother to tell me my muscles are fat.

I'll be old when I want to be, not a day sooner.
I've passed a half century by thinking young
I can do anything I did twenty years ago...
There are places to go and songs to be sung

Old is a figment of tired imagination...
Old is when I've got nowhere to go.
Old is a ghetto, a mind set, a black hole...
Old is thinking that time is my foe.

As long as a butterfly fills me with awe,
As long as a sunrise moves me to tears
As long as my friends accept me and love me
I'll never feel old, I'll never feel fear.

How much better to treasure my time on earth
Being cheerful and happy and sharing it too
I'll be old when I want to, and not a day sooner.
I'll let you know when I'm through.

Have a Little Talk With God

When you feel sad and so depressed
Like nothing will be right again.
If life gives no peace or tranquil rest
That's the place we all have been.
It's time to have a little talk with God.

☐ If even best friends let you down
If things don't go the way they should
We all are human with built-in flaws
There is much we wish we understood.
Find a place to have a talk with God.

Lift up your eyes and open your heart.
Don't try so hard to have your way
Sometimes God knows what He wants.
He always has the final say.
Take time to have a little talk with God.

You needn't make a formal prayer,
kneel in a cathedral or a temple,
God hears our whispers as well as shouts
He makes it easy and so simple
—a quiet place to have a talk with God.

If tranquility, peace and harmony can
flourish within our hearts
We first must open our minds and souls
to let negative thoughts depart.
Have that little talk with God.

the secret

It's with almost embarrassment that I tell you my

secret to enjoying life—because it is so blindingly simple.

Enjoy little things.

THE PASSING YEARS. . .

TWELVE . . .

An in-between sort of time, the age of strange passions —of sticky sentimentality and sudden hates. The time of big brother worship and hostile indifference to parents and the authority they signify. The age of innocence— where manners, dress, dates are of little concern.

An age when the importance of life lies in showing the neighborhood boys how to climb trees, play ball, and do anything they could do—better.

The time of never wanting to grow up, the feeling that the world is standing still for you.

Too big for dolls— too young for any real experiences.

The time of waiting.

SIXTEEN. . .

A happy time. Often a very lonely time. The period of growing up—when no one will believe it or wants to believe it. The feeling of kinship to God and Nature.

The frustrating sense that all is not quite as it should be, that something is missing.

The age of high school, the world of parties and dates and first formals and secret engagements. Of standing outside of life looking in. The shedding of childlike innocence and faith in the world in exchange for freedom to use your promise of the future.

You will never be this young or this old again.

EIGHTEEN . . .

The age of wonder—the time of whys and whens. The time of dreadful seriousness and abandoned hilarity. The age our parents begin to sense an aching loss. The thrilling sense of independence —of unattachment to all that's familiar.

The time when every incident is Big and Meaningful.

The time of looking for something and not knowing what it is or where you'll find it, or if you ever will.

The time of commitment to another person—the fulfilling of all of life's promises and dreams. The joy that comes with bringing another person happiness.

The sense of goodness and well-being. Looking forward to the future.

THE TERRIBLE FORTIES . . .

A traumatic, terrifying trial by turmoil. When some snigger smugly about mid-life crisis, treating it as a game, or a silly interval in one's life not to be taken seriously. When people do that—they've never gone through it.

This is a time for retrospect, a time to look back over life—sizing it up and coming up short. Halfway through life with what accomplished, is the inevitable question. Why am I here? To what purpose? Have I done any lasting good? Have I done harm? Have I at least created a tiny void in the universe? Would my passing cause even a ripple in the life stream of those who know me?

Does anyone know me? Do I know myself?

Questions, so many questions—without answers.

END OF MID-LIFE CRISIS

Just like that, traveling from the mountaintop to the valley and to the mountaintop again. Or at least to a plateau leading back to the mountain.

Maybe a lifetime contains only one mountain. Perhaps one mountain should be enough.

Maturity comes with knowing life can never be perfect. That regrets and disappointments can pile up until there is no room to peer over the mountain to see a sunrise or a sunset, to recognize a friend or assess a relationship that has merit in comfort, peace and longevity.

The real tragedy lies in failure to acknowledge the truth and beauty of Acceptance, to cease struggling for Perfection, realizing that being human nullifies the quest for perfection, from the start.

Sometimes one needs only the descent into the valley in order to see that home is not a place, but a state of mind.

THE YEARS BEYOND . . .

The years slide by swiftly, stealthily, one by one. Where do they go? Do they pile up like little particles of sawdust inside a pencil sharpener? Do they lie around, just beneath our consciousness like rotting leaves fallen from the trees—year after passing year?

The years are no longer merely a sound of numbers placed together to form a word in the dictionary. Years begin to lose their objectivity, and it is hard to regard them impersonally, as mere marks on a calendar. They become friend or foe, black or white. There is very little gray in-between when we think of passing years, as we grow older.

I still do not understand my purpose for being on earth. I feel uneasy to think of the air, water, paper, and other things I have used during my stay here. Did I repay the earth in any way? I hope so.

Will I justify my time spent by leaving my friends with good memories, by easing the way for people I've met along the way, by helping anyone who needed me? I hope so.

The closing years bring comfort and seductive whisperings of peace—of promises to keep.

Raspberry Rainbows

How Many Rainbows Will I See?

Tell me, how many rainbows will I see

And how many sunsets am I pledged?

Will the rivers still flow on without me

And birds continue nesting in flowered hedge?

How many roads will miss my passing by?

Will the stars shine as bright without my wish?

Will long ago lovers still hear my cry,

share the loss, the pain, the loneliness?

Will roses bloom well without my touch

And children remember my happy smile?

Will friends give a thought to my passing much

And recall our laughter, our special style?

Is this to be my immortality?

Tell me, how many rainbows will I see?

Published books by Pinkie Paranya

Available in print and e books

www.pinkieparanya.com

Women of the Northlands Trilogy

RAVEN WOMAN

TIANA, GIFT OF THE MOON

SEDNA, NORTH STAR RAVEN WOMAN

SAGA OF SOURDOUGH RED

LOVE LETTERS IN THE WIND

ONE…TWO…BUCKLE MY SHOE

DEATH HAS NO DOMINION

SENORA OF THE SUPERSTITIONS

SECRETS OF SEBASTIAN BEAUMONT

PRACTICE MAKES PERFECT

AMAZON TREASURES

HERR SCHNOODLE & McBEE

LIFE IN A NUT SHELL

RASPBERRY RAINBOWS

www.pinkieparanya.com

ABOUT THE AUTHOR

Raspberry Rainbows is the culmination

of a long life of joy and contentment ...

mixed with heartaches and regrets.

I have written and published many books,

but this is my true heart from the inside out.

I hope my journey will aid you in

treasuring your own rainbows.

Made in the USA
Middletown, DE
02 December 2021